"Behind the scenes, a new gene quietly learning, thinking, gro 'keep kids in the church.' They ... trying to form followers of Christ who will be leaders in the church of tomorrow. Stephen Ingram is one of the architects of this new approach to youth ministry, and I'm grateful for his example and voice."
—Brian McLaren, Author and Activist

"Forget the growth hormones! Stephen Ingram calls everyone who cares for young people to get our hands dirty in the organic soil of student ministry. Drawing on years of experience in ministry and consulting, Stephen will help you assess the particularities of your ministry context and determine what to plant and what to prune in order to promote long-term growth and sustainability. This book is required reading for anyone seeking fresh visions for youth ministry."
— Dave Csinos, Author, Speaker, Founding President, Faith Forward

"The keen mind of Stephen Ingram permeates this book. *Organic Student Ministry* is chock-full of smart, savvy youth ministry wisdom. You won't find quick, shot-in-the-arm fixes for programming. Instead, you should read each chapter like it's a treasure chest, with a yellow highlighter ready to put each gem into pragmatic practice."
— Stephanie Caro, Author, Speaker, Senior Consultant for Ministry Architects

"Finally a student ministry book written by an honest youth minister! Stephen not only captures the beautiful and hectic mess of adolescence, but lets ministers off the performance and production hook and invites them to get down and into the students' lives. *Organic Student Ministry* is the book I wish I read 15 years ago ... but at least I can share it now."
— Tripp Fuller, Cofounder of Homebrewed Christianity podcast

"Youth ministry will only be effective in our post-Christendom culture if it is contextual. Cookie cutter ministry models no longer work—if they ever did. Rooted in years of experience as a youth worker and consultant, Stephen Ingram has assembled a collection of best practices and attitude adjustments that will nurture relational and adaptive youth ministry in whatever context you serve. If you want to cultivate a dynamic and holistic ministry with young people and adults, this book is for you."

— John W. Vest, visiting Assistant Professor of Evangelism at Union Presbyterian Seminary, Cofounder of the Progressive Youth Ministry Conference

"After reading an early draft, I knew Stephen was onto something profound. I could see immediately the authentic ring of ideas proven in the crucible of actually doing ministry week in and week out with young people. Though Stephen has already contributed quite a number of books to the youth ministry conversation, *Organic Student Ministry* introduces clearly and provocatively Stephen's innovative, signature vision for ministry. I am thrilled that, at last, Stephen's timely and distinct approach will be added to the vocabulary of those seeking to do faithful work with a new generation."

— Mark DeVries, Founder of Ministry Architects and Author of *Sustainable Youth Ministry*

"Stephen Ingram is a seasoned youth pastor who gives invaluable and practical wisdom that will help cultivate your youth ministry into a vibrant growing member of the body of Christ. From pruning dying programmatic ministries to generating new practice-based ministry experiences, Ingram will take you on a journey that is sure to enhance your youth ministry."

— Brandon K. McKoy, Author of *Youth Ministry from the Outside In: How Relationships* and *Stories Shape Identity*; Senior Pastor, New Hope Baptist Church in Gastonia, North Carolina

"In an atmosphere full of the latest youth ministry fads and methodologies comes an emerging voice with a rooted, balanced, and subversive perspective. One that reaches beyond the normal drivel, letting go of what's been done or what used to work, and embracing mystery, asking questions, and creating space for youth ministry to thrive in its own unique contexts. *Organic Student Ministry* is an essential read for anyone who is engaging with kids or youth and understands that for a ministry ecosystem to thrive, it must identify its unique makeup and build from it. Stephen Ingram isn't offering a new approach here, or even a new methodology, he is flipping youth ministry on its head and exploring a new way of being."
— Jamie Rye, Wild Goose Festival Youth Coordinator

"The art and the science of youth ministry come together with Stephen Ingram's holistic approach. There are plenty of books that promise to help you make your youth group larger. This is not one of those books. The deep, spiritual method that Ingram guides you through will help you to grow your ministry with youth. Here you will find expectant hope and faithful patience, tools that gardeners employ, interpreted for youth leaders."
— Erin Reed Cooper, Editorial Project Manager for
InsideOut Christian Resources for Outdoor Ministries

ORGANIC STUDENT MINISTRY

TRASH THE PRE-PACKAGED PROGRAMS
AND TRANSFORM YOUR YOUTH GROUP

STEPHEN INGRAM

CHALICE
PRESS

ST. LOUIS, MISSOURI

Cover design: Jesse Turri

www.chalicepress.com

Print: 9780827227583
EPUB: 9780827227590   EPDF: 9780827227606

Library of Congress Cataloging-in-Publication Data

Ingram, Stephen.
Organic student ministry : trash the pre-packaged programs and transform your youth group / by Stephen Ingram. — First [edition].
    pages cm
ISBN 978-0-8272-2758-3 (pbk.)
1. Church work with youth. 2. Church work with teenagers.
I. Title.
BV4447.I475 2015
259'.23—dc23

2015013659

Contents

The Crisis of Fast-Food Ministry

In the past 30 years, student ministry has become solidified in the establishment of ecclesial life in the American church. In this solidification and subsequent recognition, much effort, scholarship, and pragmatic study have been given to better reaching, impacting and growing student ministries. While much good has come from all of this attention, the professionalization process has brought with it a number of detrimental habits and tendencies that show up in far too many youth ministries today.

It has happened in much the same way the fast food industry has been detrimental to the health of our nation. When it is popular, cheaper, faster, easier, and so readily available, it can become our default. The same trend has happened in our student ministries.

This has played itself out most prevalently in the practice of "adopt and drop." Adopt and drop is a consumer-based pattern in which we student ministers adopt the latest trend, book, or pragmatic approach and drop it into our student ministries.

What happens is that we naively expect the new ideas to "work" without considering the specific context, tone, needs, abilities, and natural gifts that already exist in our churches. This pattern produces identity confusion, anxiety, frustration, and ultimately a student ministry that lacks coherence and sustainability.

So often youth ministers inadvertently try to "plant palm trees in Antarctica." When we take some model of student ministry that has "proven" successful and try to implement it in our context, we may or may not see success. The model may be good, even great. The problem is that just because it works in southern California does not mean it is going to work in southern Indiana. Alas, time and time again we adopt these systems and structures and drop them into our contexts with little adaptation and little regard to whether they match who we are and what we are called and equipped to do.

Organic student ministry is not a program developed in a vacuum. It is, however, an approach to student ministry that worries less about giving the right answers and more about helping you asks the right questions. The only way you can help lead a student ministry toward and into fruitful ministry is to help it grow where it is planted. In order to do this you have to know a lot more than student ministry tips and tricks. You have to dig deep in the history, the passion, the DNA, and the people of the student ministry and church. You have to create better, yet unearth and cultivate the natural ministry that the church was made to do. You have to understand yourself as the curator of this great treasure, constantly helping it speak for itself and become more of who it was created to be. Inside of these questions and this investigation, you get to bring your unique talents and gifts to enhance the ministry of the church while finding fulfillment in your own calling. This sort of ministry does not depend on you and does not revolve around you.

By most accounts, the average life of a youth minister is 18–24 months and then on to the next church. What happens is that the youth minister and the church so often join in exploitative relationships, in which each other's resources (mental, spatial, creative, financial, emotional, and temporal) are exploited by the other until these resources are drained.

Then burn-out begins. I should not have to elaborate on this because, if you have been in ministry any amount of time, you know exactly what I am talking about.

There *is* hope; there *is* another way.

After 17 years in student ministry, I cannot tell you how amazing it is to lead a ministry that is so deeply rooted in the students, parents, volunteers, and the whole church. It is amazing because I know that I am joining with and enhancing the ministry that the church is called to, and not the ministry that I want to import to the community.

By living into this model, I get to walk into work each day not feeling the weight or the anxiety of the ministry on my shoulders. I get to walk into a co-op of volunteers, clergy, staff, parents, and students as one part, one piece of the greater good of the student ministry. The weight is evenly distributed and so are the joys, the triumphs, and the celebrations.

You cannot do this sort of ministry if you are selfish. If you need your youth ministry as a confidence-builder or a glory machine, then you do not need to read any further. This is a ministry model based on generosity, trust, and community. There are places for you to shine in ministry, but not as a shooting star. In this model of ministry, you do get to be a star—but one that is a part of a greater constellation.

I can promise you this is the right kind of student ministry. It is good. And it lasts.

Yesterday was a crazy day for me and the church I serve. We had a huge junior high youth retreat, full of junior-high and senior-high small group leaders, staff, and adult volunteers. It was great. But we had to end it early. We actually ended the retreat two hours early and, at the time that we should have been on the road, I found myself in a room, sitting beside seven of the adult leaders who were on the retreat. We were at the funeral of their youth minister. Our dear friend, Leon, had passed away just a few days earlier, and we changed the schedule of the retreat at the last minute to be able to be back for his memorial service. In my mind there was no question about making this change; over half of my leaders grew up in this man's youth group. We sat in our traditional sanctuary surrounded by suits, dresses, and ties. We sat there in our long-sleeve retreat t-shirts from that weekend. We did not have time to change, and to be honest Leon would not have wanted us to. We sat and we listened to story after story from the pulpit of how important and beloved this man was and is. I sat with this group of adults wearing our retreat t-shirts realizing, in a way that I never have before, just how much youth ministry matters. I was sitting in the middle of the proof of this man's legacy. Youth group was so important to these adults that they now give their gifts to the youth of the church.

Youth ministry, good youth ministry, has very little to do with youth. If our focus is on youth, then we have missed the point. We are in the business of creating, preparing, and discipling adults. Most of them are not adults yet, but that has to be our focus. We cannot be about the business of creating a generation of youth group junkies. We have to disciple them and do the long, tough, arduous, and sometimes unsatisfying work of youth ministry that lasts. No more gimmicks, no more hype, no more filler—just the good, honest work of love and grace.

My friend and incredible youth volunteer Scott (he has four girls and is a successful businessman) sat beside me in his retreat shirt and leaned over to me before the service. "I'm not sure I'll be able to make it through the funeral of my youth minister while sitting beside my daughter's youth minister."

But he made it and it was beautiful.

What each of us realized in our own way is that our dear friend Leon is not dead. He lives. He lives among us in our conversations, our faith, and our memories. He lives, and was sitting in that room—in shirts from a retreat that he never went on.

Leon stopped being the youth minister at that church when I was eight years old, and he moved to another part of the state, but I benefit from his youth ministry even today. He lives through his youth, their service, and their commitment.

Organic youth ministry is not about youth. Organic youth ministry is about what happens long after they are young, long after they are out of their parents' homes, and long after they go on a retreat. Organic youth ministry is not something that

The Crisis of Fast-Food Ministry

is quick and flashy. Organic youth ministry lasts long after you have left the church, or, as in the case of Leon, even after you have left this earth.

Simply put, it is an approach that is not bound by region or denomination, by church size or experience. It is an approach that you can turn to in your first years of ministry and your last. I can say this because it is an approach that builds upon what is already naturally occurring and grows because it is customized for each ministry context it is planted in. Organic student ministry takes more time and effort, but in return will create long-term ministry that creates disciples, empowers adults, and lets you plant beautiful and creative ministry that will flourish for years to come.

1

Grafting In

You are 23, fresh out of college and ready to prove who you are and what you can do. You have fresh new ideas and energy, and have not been jaded by the gauntlet of church ministry. You are young and are poised to do amazing things in this church.

You are 52; you are one of the ones who has stuck it out; you have proven yourself and are moving for hopefully the last time. Your experience, maturity, and knowledge let others know that this is not your first rodeo.

You have a full-time job. It is not vocational ministry. It is not even in the church. But you felt a call, saw a need, was coerced into leading a month-long Bible study that is now a part-time job in youth ministry. You have no clue what to do, what to teach, or how to answer a lot of the questions, and are truthfully wondering how you even got to this job (that is *not* your job) anyway?!?!

1

That is where the differences end—and each of you step into that office, ready to do good, impact teenagers, and build an amazing ministry.

Then it happens.

You realize either on your own or through a rough brush with ministry reality that you did not inherit a blank slate ministry with which to create your ministry masterpiece on. You *did* inherit a broken, usually hurting, dysfunctional mess teeming with emotions, agendas, and passions. And if this was not enough of an adventure, this is only a small glimpse of the bigger mess the student ministry is both causing and shouldering from the church, the local community, and the students' relationships with God.

Any attempt to insert your agenda will likely end in one of two ways:

1. Restlessness from the natives: "This is not how [*your predecessor's name*] did it!"

2. Unhealthy dependence on you: your ideas, direction, method, etc. The operative word is *YOU,* which means *YOU* are responsible, which means *YOU* will succeed or fail by *your* own effort.

Suddenly, your exciting new ministry's "new car smell" takes on a distinctly sour aroma—a mix of old Doritos and something you are sure was tracked in on the bottom of your shoe.

Lucky you!

After a few more months of uncomfortable run-ins and a couple of angry e-mails, you could be pulling out the old resume, prepping the spouse, and beginning to search the job databases again. Or, if you are a volunteer, you could slowly fade into the background of the church or leave entirely.

But, wait... Pause and rewind.

What if you started with a patient, organic approach?

A Better Way

Some of the worst mistakes a youth minister makes are in the first few months on the job. Why, you might ask? What you do in the first year sets the tone and trajectory for the years to come. You might not hear the grumbling in the first months or even the first year, not because you have necessarily started well, but because people do not want to challenge the new girl or guy. A lot of times we come into a new program and do one of two things: we either completely uproot the current system, install our regime, and work our ministry, or we come in and practice the whole "Do not touch anything for the first year" philosophy. We are either extremely hands on or completely hands off. We are either Machiavellian, where resistance is futile, or we are like my two-year-old with Play-Doh, where the unique shades of ministry that we bring are soon so smashed together with the church that both turn into an indistinguishable blob.

Machiavelli and Play-Doh

You remember Machiavelli, right? He was the guy that wrote *The Prince,* which was a book about the art of war and ruling with an iron fist. I will never forget the first time I read this book and was thinking to myself, "Wow, I know some pastors who seem to take their cues from Machiavelli more than from Jesus." There are some approaches to youth ministry that are very similar. While it may not be a conversion-by-sword sort of approach, there are many youth ministers who do adopt the my-way-or-the-highway mentality when it comes to instituting programming, vision, and mission. This approach comes in with an understanding that the youth ministry needs a new vision, mission, and a general overhaul of the program, and we are the ones they hired to do it. So we come in, institute new language, approaches, formats, worship styles, mission focus, etc. The list can go on and on.

Here are two stories that highlight the dangers of this approach. One involves very aggressive behavior, and one is much more subtle, but both lead to catastrophic results. Story number one. New youth minister hired. Everyone was very excited, they had just come off a very rough situation where they previous leader had been involved in some scandal and they were ready for a new start. So the first night, literally after the youth minister had been there less than 48 hours, he stood up and proclaimed the new vision for the youth ministry, complete with new mission statement and of course new logo. The guy had been there for 48 hours!!! Needless to say they freaked out. He had not even shared a meal with the kids yet and he was already telling them who they were and what their focus should be. They almost ran him out of the church that night.

Story number two. She was a successful youth minister and had done really good ministry at her previous two churches. It was a good transition in, and she was learning families' names and was planning a lot of relational time with students and parents. Everything was going great until the pink sofa incident. The pink sofa was ugly. Seriously, it was hideous. Anyone in their right mind would immediately burn this thing because, every time you looked at it, it burned your retinas. She thought, "It is probably some whim purchase that then turned into a "I bet the youth group would take this as a tax write-off donation." So she moved it. She found out where the storage closet was for those sorts of items, and she moved it in one Saturday morning. Then the "pink sofa apocalypse" happened. "Where did it go?" "Who moved the pink sofa?" "This is serious; I am mad." At first, she thought they were playing with her, a sort of "let's break in the new girl" treatment. Nope. They became more and more irate and refused to start Sunday school until someone answered for their crimes. So after about 20 minutes she gave up. "I just thought it was ugly and did not match the rest of the youth room—which is impeccably decorated, by the way—so I thought I would move it." They almost ran her out of that church as well.

It turns out that, in both instances, one intentional and the other unintentional, these two youth ministers dramatically disturbed the homeostasis of the ministries they came to help. Both, with the best intentions at heart, made the fatal flaw of approaching their respective ministries with a Machiavelli-like lens and subsequently started off their ministries with these churches on very shaky ground.

The other side of the coin is the Play-Doh approach. The Play-Doh approach is much less aggressive, but just as damaging. Here's another story. Michelle, a gifted young woman started her first youth ministry job. Although it was her first job in youth ministry, it was certainly not her first professional experience. She had spent the past six years as a professional systems crisis counselor. Her job was to go into and work with businesses that were having personnel problems and help them resolve the problems in an amicable manner while at the same time creating better systems that, if followed, would help alleviate and prevent crises in the future.

Crazy enough, she felt a calling into youth ministry and jumped into it, leading youth part time while keeping her other job. The church she began to work with was one she had been worshiping with and she was very excited about the opportunity. This church, like many others, had had it's fair share of crises over the past ten years, some of which Michelle had been made aware of before she took the job. While the turmoil was not overwhelming, it was definitely affecting the ministries. When Michelle was hired, she tried to fly low. Although she knew that she had skills and experience that could be very useful with the turmoil and confusion, she continued to not insert herself into the unhealthy systems that were eating at her church. She simply melded herself into the church, kept a low profile, and watched the systems continue to produce very unhealthy fruit. Her unique gifts went unnoticed, unused, and were consequently unhelpful. She became indistinguishable. Her unique abilities never showed through, and she began to feel like Play-Doh in a child's hands.

Let me pause here and distinguish between becoming Play-Doh and becoming part of a community. In community, you do adopt similar practices and traits. It does not mean that you become indistinguishable. When you become a part of a community, you do not lose the things that make you you. You add things that keep you identifiable, unique, and wholly distinct. Think of a salad: tomatoes, lettuce, carrots, etc. If you just throw these in a bowl, they are a lot of individual parts. But together, with or without dressing, they become a salad. You do not put everything into a blender so that all the items are turned into an indistinguishable puree; that would be gross and not a salad. Each part is still distinguishable, but together they make a salad..

A Third Way: The Way of St. Patrick

There is another way. There is an alternative to either "conquering and assimilating" or "becoming an indistinguishable gelatinous blob" in ministry. It is the way of St. Patrick. St. Patrick lived around 1600 years ago and, believe it or not, provided a pretty incredible model for how to peacefully move into a church community and at the same time maintain your gifts, personality, and integrity.

In order to understand this technique, you first have to understand Patrick's backstory. According to *The Confession of St. Patrick,* Patrick, as a 16-year-old, was abducted from his homeland of Great Britain and taken as a slave to Ireland. He was there for six years, until he escaped and fled back to Great Britain. He followed a call into the ministry and spent the following years studying theology and becoming ordained as a priest.

Upon the completion of his training, he was sent back to Ireland. Patrick had a couple of options at this point. He could have gone in with dogged determination to eradicate anything that did not fit into his belief structure and practice, or he could go in and adhere to the already established norms of Christianity.

He chose neither.

Neither made sense.

He was not going to go in and completely destroy their way of life and demand that they convert to his understanding of the faith. At the same time, he knew that they needed something else, something more than what they were currently experiencing.

So he chose a third way.

One of the things that makes Patrick unique is he chose to help the people of Ireland, both pagan and Christian, understand the faith in their own terms, using their own symbols and practices, and even their own holy days. The predominant religious group, the druids, had beliefs, practices, and holy days that were not only central to their way of life but also reflected the way of life of the people of Ireland. Patrick had experienced the way of life, customs, and rituals of the druids as a prisoner for six years, so he knew them well. They were not just a group of pagans who, as it would have seemed to an outsider, worshiped the sun and burned sacrificial piles of wood. He knew that these were devoted people, people who believed in what they did and were children of the living God.

Patrick did not look at them as people below himself or as people whom he would "set straight," saving them from their religious folly. He first sought to understand them, to know them, and live among them. Patrick lived in a tension that is not foreign to many youth ministers. He knew if he completely assimilated into the culture then he would never be able to make a difference in it. At the same time, he also knew there would be a time when the principles of his faith and the practices of the druids would collide. He knew when that time came he would have to be ready, he would have to be trusted, and he would have to make a strong yet calibrated move to show that the God he served was different from the deities of the druids.

So, what's a saint to do?

In life and ministry, there are some things you'll recognize and feel at home with, and others that seem blatant contradictions to the way you believe God is calling both you and the church.

So what do you do?

Do you uproot everything to plant something new? Or do you do nothing and hope it works out for the best? Either one could have you looking for another new job in 9–12 months.

Listening and Responding

First, listen and observe. You are not a deity. You do not have all of the answers and you are not the savior of the world or even this church. While you do have a lot to bring to this church, the church also has a lot to teach you. Seriously, even the most messed up churches have something to teach each of us. Sometimes they teach us by helping us learn what not to do, but no matter what we can still learn from them.

Listening requires less talking. For many of us this can be one of the hardest parts of this job. Listen for their fears. They are fearful, at least in some part. They want to be better, they want to do something more, but at best are fearful of their own inefficiencies, failures, and their own pasts. Also, listen for their dreams. I will guarantee you that they have dreams; you might have to mine them out, but they are there. If it seems like there are a lack of dreams, it might even be that you have to help them remember that they are allowed to dream. I experience this with a lot of churches. They have not only forgotten their dreams but many have forgotten how to dream.

Now, you might be thinking, "Well, Stephen, why don't you ask them about who they are, their programs, their current leadership, what has been working well, etc.?" You could do that, but usually you are going to get some stylized, sanitized understanding of self that reflects more of who they think they should be or, even worse, more reflective of who they think you want them to be. That is not what we are after; those responses only reflect what they believe is expected, not necessarily who they have been created to be as the church. When you ask for and listen to dreams and fears, you move past the shell of what should be and into the core of what could be. It is in our dreams and fears, these more primal of places, that we find the best hope for what God can do in the life of a congregation as well as in the life of an individual.

As you listen, take notes and look for themes and patterns. They are there, they just have to be recognized and brought to the surface. These patterns will tell you not only where they have been but where they are feeling called to go. You will become the holder of this collective dream and the custodian of its preservation and, ultimately, its birth.

You have a unique place and ability to do this. Not only are you new, so you're impartial, but you also have a clearer slate to hear these true and vulnerable hopes.

These are your treasures. Guard them as such.

Sort

Not everything you hear will have equal value. You have to make some judgment calls. Don't make the mistake of believing that everything you hear is something you have to enact. There will be both fears and dreams that will rise to the surface to focus on. Sort, prioritize, and reflect back to the people of the congregation what you have learned. This does a few things. The first is that it shows that you have listened to them. Few things will go further in your ministry than when people know they have been listened to. Second, it will give them a common purpose and some commonly understood baselines from which to work. Last, it gives the people in your congregation something to work on and with, together.

The best functioning churches and the best functioning youth ministries are the ones that have some common goals, purposes, and projects to work on and with together. This is a great gift you can give them.

Align

This is when you and your gift sets finally come into the picture. At six to nine months into your position, this is the first time you should begin to assert yourself in your position as leader of the ministry. This is where you get to align your gifts, strengths, and passions with the ministry that has been defined by the congregation, parents, and youth.

Look at the priorities that have been defined and ask yourself, "Where do I fit in?" This should not be a one-time question that you ask in your ministry. It must be the question that you ask again and again. It is so important to remember that the ministry you are doing is not "your" ministry and the church is not "your" church. The ministry that you get to lead is a ministry that you have been entrusted to take care of, curate, and maximize. It is the ministry of God through this particular part of the church.

The most common problem many youth ministers and clergy have is that they align the church to their mission instead of the other way around. Remember these two simple and humbling facts: they asked you to join them and, long after you are gone, they will still be there. Let this encourage you that the complete responsibility for the success of this ministry does not fall upon you. You are a piece in the wonderful puzzle that's emerging.

Refine

After you have aligned your gifts, passions, and self to the ministry your church is being called to, you must look for gaps in that ministry. While the process of listening and observing will give you a great picture of the future of the ministry of the church, it will have some holes. None of us as individuals are completely self-aware, and the same rule also applies to the church. As you look over the landscape of ministry you should now be looking for two things: (1) Where are the gaps? and (2) Where is the overgrowth?

First, the gaps. I was consulting with a church a few years ago and we were doing a time of visioning and mission setting. It was a great process and, as we came around to the end of the brainstorming of the goals and mission, everyone was very excited, pleased, and feeling really good about the impressive list of future possibilities. I felt good about them too: Bible studies, new facilities, trips, parent involvement, discipleship, etc.

That is, I did feel good until I went back to my hotel that night and began looking over the list from a 30,000-foot view. As I considered the topics on the list I noticed one glaring thing: there was no mention of mission or outreach—not one soup kitchen, no homeless shelter, no blanket drives, and no mission trips. Nothing. This is problematic in itself. It is even more problematic as one of the primary words in the church's mission statement was "serve."

When I went back the next day, I told the group that we had a problem. After going through their goals and pointing out the massive gap, they were mortified. We quickly jumped back into brainstorming and rectified the problem. We came out with some outstanding ideas for how they could better reach out to their community and "the least of these."

The problem is clear. If I hadn't gone back and looked at it from an objective point of view, we might have missed this incredibly important piece of ministry. In this process you will have to step back at times all along the way and continually ask yourself, *Where are the holes? Where are there gaps in this ministry?*

Next, the overgrowth. Churches are bad, I mean really bad, at cutting overgrowth.

"That is who we are!"

"It would not be [enter name of church] if we did not do that program!"

"We have always done it that way."

This last one is maybe the most dreadful of the most common phrases that keep churches and youth ministries from cutting or refining programs that no longer align with the mission or values of the ministry. Ministries are notorious for keeping programs alive because of what they *were,* and not because of what they currently are. You will not only have to look for and recognize the gaps in the ministry but you will also have to look for the overgrowth that will choke out new growth. (We will explore this more in the next chapter on "weeds" and "wildflowers.")

Activate

Finally comes that time to do something. I know it seems like a long time coming, but you have finally laid the groundwork to do the ministry of the church, *not* the ministry of the minister. For many people this is the most difficult part of the plan. It is the most difficult because this is where we go beyond the theoretical, the meetings, the dreaming, and the talk, and into the hard work, sweat, and time. As you get ready to activate your new mission and vision, there are two major pitfalls to avoid.

Analysis Paralysis

This is not a term I coined. I'm not sure where it came from, but it is one of the biggest contributors to atrophy in the beginning phases of new ministries.

People want a plan. This is good. People want a good plan. This is even better. But when people want a perfect plan, this is insanity. There are no perfect plans. Trust me. There are only plans that continually move toward or away from perfection, failing or succeeding toward greater excellence.

Your plan, no matter how hard you work, pray, and analyze, will not be perfect. Release yourself and your plan from this unrealistic expectation. It is so easy for a vision or plan to become trapped in the deadly cycle of analysis. At some point you will have to simply activate and begin the healthy process of trying, failing, adjusting, and retrying.

Part of doing this well is setting everyone up with the same expectations. Make sure that everyone knows that everything we do falls into this process and that each time we fail and adjust we become better and more aligned with the mission that God is calling us to.

Wait for Growth

I know it seems like a lot of work, and it is. It would be a lot easier to just come in and spend time with youth and parents, do some good activities, lead Bible studies, and see where it goes. It could go really well! It could also go really poorly. You do still need to do the Bible studies, the games, the relationships, and all of those other things that were the reasons you probably got into youth ministry. Those are good and great things. There is also this other side, though. There is the side of ministry that plans not only for next week but for the next generation. You want to be at a church for a long time, trust me. You want to see your sixth graders through graduation and beyond. You want to be able to look back over a long line of relationships, successes, and even failures. Longevity is not a bonus in youth ministry; it is becoming more and more apparent that it is a necessity. Starting well in student ministry is one of the only ways to do this. A ministry that is developed as a culmination of the partnership between the youth minister, the volunteers, the parents and the whole church will always be so much better than anything that you or I could do by ourselves.

Distinguishing the Wildflowers
from the Weeds

There are a hundred incarnations of the old saying, "One man's trash is another man's treasure." While each of these sayings are contextualized, they all have the central message: "What you consider valuable is all about perspective." I will add my contextualized voice to the myriad that have preceded it by coining "One person's weeds are another person's wildflowers."

Okay, that is sort of a lie. I thought I made that up until I did a search of the phrase and saw that Susan Wittig Albert coined it in her 2003 work *An Unthymely Death and Other Garden Mysteries*. While that is neither here nor there, I want to give credit where credit is due.

My what-I-thought-to-be original saying came to me in the long, hot, dog days of a Southern summer in 2006.

I have always had a sort of love/hate relationship with grass.

When it is bright green, perfectly cut, and free of weeds, the love abounds. The rest of the time (usually 98 percent of the time) I find myself in the constant battle of cutting, aerating, feeding, watering, and weeding, hoping for that beautiful, naturally lush carpet of green goodness. In the southeastern U.S., one of the primary enemy combatants in the "battle of the grass" is the evil prickly Sow Thistle. I know plants cannot be evil, so it might seem a little dramatic, but, seriously, this robust, indignant, sturdy weed was the bane of my backyard. It would not only grow fast, it would grow tall. If I were busy for a few weeks and not able to take care of that area of the yard, that stuff would take up residence—and in an impressive way.

There was one instance of Sow Thistle I remember particularly well. It grew just outside our bedroom window and at the perfect angle so every morning when I woke up, it would raise its spiny head to the edge of the window and stare at me taunting me. It had a look to say, "I'm here, still here, and I am not going away, sucker."

I really hated this weed.

Then something happened.

I came home one afternoon and my wife told me she had finished a new painting. Of course, I told her I could not wait to see it and I followed her to her art desk—and there it was: the evil Sow Thistle stood there, in careful brushstrokes, staring at me. The Sow Thistle had wooed my wife and was now in my home.

I don't advise using my first reaction, especially if the painter's your wife: "Why in the world would you paint a weed? I hate weeds."

In her generous way (one she has developed masterfully after being married to me for so many years), she responded, "I think it's nice. I like it, so I painted it. It is not a weed; it is a wildflower and I think it's pretty." I took a step back and, in a moment, I forgot my tumultuous history with said weed and saw it in an entirely new light. She was right. There were purples and deep greens, yellow flowers that looked like dandelions, and thousands upon thousands of these paper-thin translucent needles reaching out in every direction. It was strong yet delicate, intimidating yet inviting. Magically, my perspective shifted. I now saw *both* sides of the Sow

Thistle. It was nuisance or beauty or both, depending on one's perspective.

In youth ministry there are a lot of these weed/wildflower conundrums. There will always be those situations, programs, events, and ministries of which we have to ask those discerning questions. When we inherit a ministry, and all ministries are inherited, we receive treasures, traps, and a whole lot of weedy wildflowers.

The tension we will consistently find ourselves in is how to determine what parts of the ministry are weeds, which are wildflowers, and how to deal with both once we determine what they are.

No matter how we go about this, the moral of the story is that many of these things we will talk about are *both* weeds and wildflowers. Part of our discernment is realizing that so much depends on perspective and context, neither of which will we always know right away.

Ripping Out Wildflowers

I could share many stories in which I have seen others, and myself for that matter, tear out beds of wildflowers, mistaking them for weeds. However, one stands out in particular.

I knew this guy who had moved to his dream church. This church was one of those great situations in which he and the church seemed to be a perfect fit. He had been working at the church for about three months when he decided some changes needed to be made. This church had a long tradition of really meaningful small groups that not only developed excellent community but also helped this fairly large church feel smaller. The new guy had worked at churches where small groups were important and were a central part of the DNA; this is yet another reason why it seemed to be a perfect fit for the youth minister and the church.

The only problem is that the youth minister had done small groups in a different way than the way the church had set up. The youth minister was used to having more control of the content, set up, and organization of the small groups. The groups at the church formed more naturally, usually around friends. The new youth minister wanted to change this system. Not only did he not feel comfortable with the system in place, he also did not know how to manage it.

So at first he began to try to assert more control over the groups and began adding more structures and oversight to the groups. While I am usually very much for these sorts of system overhauls, it was obvious that it was coming across heavy-handed and the groups began to resent his involvement. Soon it became evident that their groups were not going to fall in line with the new systems. The new youth minister became more and more frustrated that they were not following his leadership, until one day about eight months into his new job he announced that the youth group would no longer have small groups and that they had become somewhat of an idol for the group.

Needless to say, this did not sit well with the youth and parents of the congregation. About six months later, just over a year into the job, the new youth minister left. He had lost the trust, respect, and following of his group.

Do not rip out wildflowers mistaking them for weeds. Just because it feels like a nuisance to you does not mean that you should—or even have the right to—eliminate it.

While keeping that warning in the forefront of your mind I want to also acknowledge that there are weeds in every ministry. There are those programs, traditions, and even leaders that are deeply rooted and detrimental to the overarching vision and execution of the ministry. Here are three questions to ask to determine what are the wildflowers or weeds growing in your ministry.

Codependency or Healthy Co-beneficial Relationships?

Unfortunately, some people, at some times, can be weeds. In unhealthy circumstances they can be weeds to a ministry. One of the most prevalent ways is when they are codependent with the ministry or students.

Codependency happens when people try to meet their emotional and psychological needs through the ministry or in their relationships. This is a good place for some self-evaluation.

I was working with a church several years ago that had a guys ministry. At least, that's what it seemed to be from the outside. These guys would get together once a week in a few groups and would just pour their hearts out to one another. There were tears, deep sharing, and a very strong sense of community. That is, until a new youth minister tried to probe a little deeper and bring them under the vision and authority of the church. Almost immediately the leader resisted. The guys would stop coming, he said. They would no longer feel safe and their needs would no longer be met. The unreasonably strong response caused us to dig deeper, at which point, two things became evident.

The leader had an unhealthy attachment to the dynamic of the group, and most of the guys were coming out of a sense of obligation to this leader, to support him and to be faithful to him. Again, if you looked at the attendance and satisfaction level, you would think this was a healthy ministry. But below the surface was a toxicity that was engrained and growing.

The opposite is a ministry that is co-beneficial, in which both the leaders and the participants can be ministered to and minister within. I have a volunteer who is an excellent example of this. He has a calling to minister with students. It is not a need, it is a calling that his life be shared with the students in our ministry. He is not emotionally dependent; his well-being is not based on the well-being of the students. He has the ability to be in those tough situations with students and at the same time to rise above those situations—not being sucked into their immediate problems, but able to see their lives with perspective and provide hope. Codependents cannot function this way. In codependent relationships, participants become enmeshed and feed off each others' feelings. They cannot rise above circumstances and are unable to find perspective that leads to hope. If you find yourself or your leaders unable to achieve perspective apart from your students' situations, or you or your leaders feel caught up emotionally in the situations and problems of your students, take a step back. Empathy *is* good and, for students who are hurting, it is vital. However, what often happens is an adult begins to develop a need to be the "savior" for the students. Instead of being an objective agent of healing, some adults unknowingly use a relationship to feel better about themselves. This is selfish, wrong, and dangerous. There is a world of difference between standing in the gap for someone and wallowing in the mud with them—and it all comes down to motive. If you know of or are in unhealthy relationships, you need to recognize any selfish purposes and establish a firm line in place of the one that has become blurred. Spend any time at all in ministry and you will have to deal with this weed. It's inevitable. People are human and codependency is in every church.

Does It Overtake and Prevent Other Growth?

One of the most damaging things about weeds is that they overtake and root out other plants around them. They stress and deplete resources, time, and energy at rates that are harmful and irresponsible to the growth around them. The same thing happens in ministries. Most youth ministries—and churches for that matter—have at least one of their programs that sucks the life, resources, and energy from the rest of the ministry. They are usually run by a dedicated leader, who is often the founder of that program or has a close emotional tie to it. For them it *is* the ministry. Sometimes it is a fundraiser; other times it is a trip or a mission project. The problem is not the program or ministry itself. In other contexts it might function very well and even become the healthy centerpiece of that ministry. The problem comes when its existence and perpetuation becomes detrimental and even harmful to the overarching goals and vision of the ministry in which it exists. If other ministries have to function in spite of it, you might have a problem.

An example is a fundraiser that I witnessed at a church one time. It was designed to help the youth ministry raise funds for their annual mission trip. In its early days it was incredibly beneficial. It did its job and brought energy to the group and the congregation. Soon its success became overwhelming. The fundraiser became more and more complicated, needing more and more people and more and more resources. Soon it was taking up massive slots on the calendar and was ultimately wearing everyone out, including the beneficiaries of the funds. It was no longer functioning as it should and had become a beast in and of itself that, like the plant in *Little Shop of Horrors,* had an insatiable appetite, constantly begging the church for one more bite.

In our best-case scenarios each of our ministries function alongside each other in mutually beneficial ways. When these are at their best they are united by a common mission and goal. They each, in their own way, seek to help the ministry achieve that overarching goal as well as complement each other.

Have you even seen a cornfield? If you have you will notice just how close the stalks are planted together; it is amazing just how many are on a single row. The reason farmers do this is because each stalk needs other stalks close so that they can cross-pollinate. They do not push each other out. They actually help each other and grow because of what the other does. In our best incarnations, our programs and ministries should work in the same ways.

Complementary Crops or Single-Focus Landscaping?

It is good to know who you are, what you are good at, and the unique niche you are called to fill in the greater scope of Christianity. Too often the problem comes when we find ourselves only being one type of church or group and completely neglecting the other pieces of the faith that we are called to live and strengthen.

We see it all of the time. The youth group is all about worship music and will sing for hours, but rarely will you see them taking care of the poor. Another group is all about deep study, learning about and working on the major social ills of its community, yet they will rarely if ever talk about the Jesus who calls them to do these things. Still others will focus on getting as many kids through the doors of the church, but will end up rarely giving them anything substantive enough to provide the growth to become dedicated disciples of Jesus.

All churches do it. All groups do it. Granted, it is to varying degrees, but this is something we are all guilty of. The best groups are aware of this and are constantly pushing themselves to make sure there is growth and sustainability in ways that are not their default sweet spots of ministry. None of us are called to have a single, solitary focus. We cannot show the world our God by only giving them a solitary glimpse at one of God's attributes. If you are a group that has nine Bible studies a week and one time of serving others a month, you might want to rethink your programming. If you are spending loads of your time and budget on your worship time, but do not live out or understand worship as something that we have the opportunity to do with our whole lives, music or not, you might want to reevaluate your allotments. If you are the group that is so serious all of the time with study and thought that you forget to have fun and be a community of joy, you might want to take a deep breath and rediscover the other aspects that tie your community together.

This does not mean that if you are a group that finds a lot of its identity around worship that you should stop or even cut it dramatically. It just means that you also have to make sure that your students understand that singing in a service is not the central mark of their faith. We as caretakers of these students must expose them to a broad array of practices and incarnations of the faith that will help them know that God and the whole of the Christian faith is much bigger than whatever it is that we tend to focus on the most. Just remember that even our most dominant "plant," the one that grows most naturally in our church's soil, can at times become problematic and even act as a weed when it goes unmanaged and is not properly balanced.

Is it a weed or a wildflower? Is it harmfully spreading or merely growing at incredible rates? Is it healthy ministry or a problem to be dealt with? None of these are questions with easy, clean-cut answers. There are always anomalies and exceptions. There are always instances in which the lines are more blurred than definitive. No matter what decisions we make about the programs and ministries that these questions are asked of, we must remember to prune and cultivate with care and compassion.

These programs and ministries mean something to someone or else they would probably not be there. Contrary to the analogies in this book, ministry is not as easy as a garden. It is complicated and has way more intertwined roots below the surface, which we will rarely if ever see. Ultimately, we are not dealing with a ministry or a program, we are dealing with people. So, as you venture into this weeding process in your ministry, do so with love. Do so with understanding and do so with absolute gentleness and love. Unlike a garden, where you can make a mistake and pluck a wildflower, some things will not just grow back.

Be gentle, be patient, and be kind.

3

"Locavore" Student Ministry

I live in the South.

It is an interesting place.

It has some of the best food in the world—with many "loca-vore" restaurants that serve only locally grown food. It's a concept that's gained a lot of traction as our culture becomes more health conscious. I'd like to relate it to student ministry a bit here.

The South has a natural beauty and, of course, its own very interesting vernacular. We are known for our long, drawn-out accents as well as the Southern hospitality that is communicated using all of those extra syllables.

People, like the tea, are very sweet. That part is true. Drivers wave when you pass, "Please" and "Thank you" are common, and there is a sense, at least from surface interactions, that people do not see you as an obstacle (unless you are in traffic in Atlanta on I 285).

Beware, though! Not everything is as it seems.

There are certain words and phrases that you must be aware of and know they have a double meaning.

Quick test:

A. Have you ever been in a conversation with a person from the South and they tell you a juicy piece of gossip and say that it is so you can be in prayer for the situation?

B. Have you ever had a person, many times older than you, find out something about you that they may not approve of and their reply or comment is, "Well bless your heart"?

If so, you probably know the importance of the subtext of these seemingly benign words. If you have spent any time at all in my neck of the woods you know that when someone is telling you gossip, it is not for prayer—it is for gossip! Also, if you have ever heard the words, "Well, bless your heart," in that context you know without a doubt that you are not being blessed; you are being talked down to. Again, unless you are culturally fluent, these things will go completely unnoticed and you will miss the subtle yet very important nuances of the language.

Church languages are like this. Each church has its own unique, subtle language—sayings and inflections that you must not only be aware of but become fluent in.

I was working in a certain church early in my youth ministry career that was in a lower middle class working part of town. The church was what I call a polar church: it had youth, and it had older people, and not much in-between the poles. It was also the case that the two poles were pretty frigid toward one another.

One day one of the older members of the congregation, a staunch member of one of the poles, asked if he could talk with me. We proceeded to have a very nice conversation about how he and his Sunday school class wanted to volunteer to help paint the youth room. After I picked my jaw up off of the floor, I smiled, thanked him, and told him that I looked forward to talking about those possibilities.

After church I mentioned the offer to one of the families at lunch. I told them of the generous offer by one of the older Sunday school classes and how excited I was about them finally warming up to the youth ministry.

Suddenly a panicked look came over both the youth and the dad's face. "When did he say they were going to paint it?" the dad asked frantically. I told them we had not decided on a date and were going to talk about it later. The dad immediately picked up his cell phone and started making calls. After a few minutes he came back and told me this class had been "at war" with the youth group for the past three years about the color of the youth room. By the way, the room was painted black with white crosses, with a very cool and well-done abstract Jesus on the wall. It was the only room in the church that was not circa 1968. This class was very angry because they believed the youth room should match the rest of the church and they had not been consulted when the change was made (though the church leadership had given their blessing).

Apparently they had been trying for years to figure out a way to get the youth room back to the "inviting" shade of muted mustard yellow the rest of the church was bathed in. As the new, young youth minister, I was their ticket. I also found out they'd planned a painting party that afternoon so it would be done quickly and no one could object. We were literally two to three hours from "muted mustard"–Gate.

Why? Because I did not know the language.

In ministry, you not only have to know the language, you also have to know the language behind the language.

There is a local dialect and culture. And you need to learn to speak it if you hope to influence it.

And the best way is to pay attention to the locals.

Spin Artists, Ringmasters, and Storytellers

You need to get over it; you are in the PR game.

You have to help the congregation see the whole picture of the youth, not just the broken window.

Knowing the language and the language behind the language is only the first part. You also have to know how to be the chief public relations officer for the youth ministry.

Now, I know what you are probably thinking: *I did not get into youth ministry to sell things. I just want the church to love the group for who they are. Isn't it dishonest to spin it?*

I get it. And I agree. But here is the problem: You know these kids—their problems, struggles, successes, intentions, and, ultimately, their hearts. When a kid breaks a chair accidentally, you know it was an accident and that he feels really bad about it. When a youth is caught walking outside of the church during service, you know she probably just needed to get away for a few moments and was not causing anyone any harm. You also know that the water all over the floor in the bathroom was caused by a water fight between three jr. high boys and they should not have done that.

You know the back stories.

You know the reasons.

You know the kids.

Your congregation does not, and they are not going to.

That is why your job as a PR specialist is so important. There are three examples of how a youth minister can do this that will not only keep the ministry in good standing with the members of the congregation, it will also help point them to what really matters in your ministry.

The Spin Artist

Spin Artist: a person (such as a political aide) whose job involves trying to control the way something (such as an important event) is described to the public in order to influence what people think about it.

The Spin Artist is probably the most controversial of the three roles I am asking you to play, so let's talk about it first.

I used to love the show *Spin City*. It was about the New York City mayor's office and its crew of publicity "spinners." They were constantly working to make the best of the mayor's negative actions, and suggest they were actually positives. It was hilarious (and, for a kid who grew up in the 80s, seeing Michael J. Fox and Cameron from *Ferris Bueller's Day Off* on the same show was magic!).

Reality check: If you are in youth ministry (which I assume you are, since you are reading this book) then you know that there are going to be times, maybe lots of times, where you have situations that need a little "reshaping" in order for people to understand that, even when the police are called, good ministry is still taking place.

I was 17, and my youth minister had just bought a new smoke machine. I am still not sure why we needed the super high-powered industrial convert grade model... but I digress. It was late and there were still a few of us hanging out at the church with our youth minister. We all, including the youth minister, decided it would be a good idea to go up to the youth room and see just how powerful this new smoke machine really was—"product research." We went into the youth room, which was on the third floor, and proceeded to pump it with as much smoke as the machine would put out. I can say the church got their money's worth with this machine. Within ten minutes, the room was a thick cloud of bluish white smoke. We decided to up the ante and turn off all the lights and shine stage lights through the smoke. The blue looked the coolest. It was awesome. That is, until three policemen stormed into the room, guns drawn, demanding answers to their questions of who we were and what were we doing there.

Good PR for youth ministry, right? Not if you happened to drive by the church that night and wondered why a SWAT team was invading your church! By the next week, most everyone had heard the news. That story needed a little spinning. Not deception, no lies, just a little context and details. The truth of the matter is that, during nights like those, I found my calling into ministry. On nights like those, my soul was nourished and bonds were solidified. On nights like those I learned how to be a youth minister.

Now, I do not do that kind of thing in my youth ministry. For one thing, I make sure to be home with my family on the majority of nights. But I learned the importance of relationships and unplanned time. My youth minister did not spin it very well. The truth is that we had been discussing the youth group and how to minister to it more effectively. The problem was that without that context the youth room looked like it was on fire and the cops thought the arsonists were still in the building.

Spin is not lying. The sort of spin I am condoning here is helping people see the fuller picture of truth and the silver lining in each situation.

One word of caution: If you cannot readily identify the deeper purpose or the silver lining and feel comfortable with it, then you should probably evaluate what you are doing. Do not allow yourself or youth in situations that are only going to get you into trouble.

Another story: Same church, same youth minister, same me. We had just discovered Ultimate Frisbee, and we were obsessed. But it was raining and we'd planned to play. So, my youth minister thought long and hard about somewhere we could throw the Frisbee on this cold, rainy night. We did not have a gym and the ceiling was too low in the fellowship hall so he made the call that we could throw it in our sanctuary.

You know—the sanctuary with the high ceilings, big chandeliers, and beautiful stained-glass windows. Yeah, that sanctuary. We had a blast. Throwing from the balcony, the pulpit, the back row, everywhere.

It was awesome.

Until it wasn't.

Sure enough, one stray throw and the sound of breaking glass. We had a problem.

It was not a whole window, just a 2 x 2 inch section. No big deal, right? Actually it was about a $900 big deal. We all got into trouble for that one. There was no silver lining. We had good conversations about responsibility, yes. We found fellowship, yes. But could these things have only come through throwing a Frisbee in the sanctuary?

Be ready to spin. But do not spin bad choices. Being a youth minister will, by itself, give you plenty of opportunities to tell the positive side of a seemingly negative story. Don't help create negative buzz. It will come on its own.

The Ringmaster

The Ringmaster: the one who helps reveal what is most important to the audience and creates anticipation for what is to come; the important manager of the performance, and the guide.

Before modern lighting equipment, it was the ringmaster's job to literally direct the attention of the audience to the appropriate sections of the performance area as the previous act was being removed or the next act was being set up in another area. The ringmaster was responsible for maintaining the smooth flow of the show—or at least the appearance of it.

He could often have to adjust to the unexpected quickly, filling time if an act was not ready.

The ringmaster is a pretty complicated job that has a very simple result. The ringmaster is charged with making sure that everyone's eyes are focused in the right direction, while making sure the transition is smooth when it is time to look at something else.

If your ministry is anything like mine, there are a lot of moving parts. It is important to communicate all of these parts well and efficiently, but that is not the job of the ringmaster. The ringmaster helps the audience (the rest of the church who are not parents or volunteers) focus on a couple of things at a time that showcase the best of what the youth ministry is doing at any given time, while providing the desired narrations that help shape what the viewer is seeing. The congregation does not need to know that Bible study is Wednesday at 6:00 p.m. That is for parents, students, and volunteers. The congregation needs to see those things that tell them the insuring essentials of what the ministry is doing.

Instead of telling the congregation that this semester you will study the gospel of John on Sunday nights, help them see the bigger scope of the plan the youth ministry has for study this year. Show them the intentionality of what you are doing and the great people you have to help lead these studies.

Instead of telling them that you are taking the kids to this big retreat this fall, help them understand how retreats and mission trips play into the spiritual development of the group, and why that is an essential part of the ministry that you are doing.

Instead of telling them how incredibly the youth worshiped at the big youth worship concert Saturday night, help the youth incorporate into the leadership of the Sunday morning worship in meaningful and visible ways.

Too often youth ministry is something seen as a "behind the curtain" ministry. There is often this sense that the congregation knows something is happening back there, but is not sure what, and is definitely not sure of the purpose. The job of the ringmaster is to put the important parts out front for all to see and narrate why they are important. When this is done well no one notices the messy work of setting up the next ring, or even if the elephant left a few presents on his way out of the last performance!

The Storyteller

The Storyteller: a person who has a special way of telling stories and anecdotes that not only draws the audience in but convinces them that they too are a part of the story.

If I am being honest, this is my favorite role to play. It is my favorite form of communication. I love stories that draw me in and take me to another place.

Jesus was a storyteller. In a way, "spinning" and "ring-mastering" well are complimentary components of being good storytellers.

Of course, any story is limited. Your listeners can't feel the adrenaline pulsing through your veins—as you felt in the moment. They won't have the same sensory overload as you had, and you processed things differently than they will hearing your version later. But you can still help bring the hearers into the story and compensate for some of those gaps, helping listeners get the "truth" of the story instead of some sterile facts.

With stories, you can help to create the "language" of your church.

You can talk about your ministry with numbers, programs, and in generalities, but when you bring all of that into a real and personal story, people listen. Stories bring your congregation into the center of your ministry from right there in their pews. Stories lift the shrouds of mystery that many feel cover youth ministry and reveal deep, heart-warming experiences that transform lives and shape students.

In order to do this, we must be storytellers and create storytellers. Being a storyteller takes only two simple steps.

1. *Always look.* There is always a story waiting to be told. It just has to be uncovered. If you do not have eyes that are intentionally looking, you might miss some pretty incredible moments.

It was a normal Saturday volunteer workday for the youth. It was a small crowd. We had a couple of staff, three other adult leaders, and around 12 youth. Again, very normal. The group was reroofing a shed for an elderly woman. The leader of the project, a dedicated youth volunteer in his mid-seventies we lovingly knew as Mr. Mac; Laura, a dedicated adult volunteer; and her seventh-grade daughter Hannah were working on the pinnacle of the roof. Laura looked up and said to Mr. Mac, "You know, I think I worked on this roof when I was in youth group." Mr. Mac smiled and said, "You are right. You did. Actually, we did." As they talked, Mr. Mac reminded her that he taught her how to put on shingles for the first time on that very same roof 20 years ago. It occurred to Laura that her daughter, brand new to the youth group, was learning on the very same roof that she did when she was in youth group. One roof, 20+ years, three generations, and a few shingles make for one incredible story. I use this story to talk about a number of important aspects of our ministry: the importance of volunteering, long-term volunteers, parents volunteering with their children, missions, long-term commitments to short-term missions, how we are never too old to volunteer, and so on.

It does not take miraculous events—just an eye for the nicely packaged, everyday, meaningful stories that paint a picture of the ministry you do with students.

2. *Build your collection.* Mark Twain was known for having an appropriate story for every situation. I remember being a kid and listening to this old man in our town. He was amazing. No matter what the situation, he could always pull an interesting, succinct, and relevant story from his hat. I determined at a very young age I wanted to be that sort of person when I grew up.

It was very frustrating for me in the weeks, months, and years after that decision. I always saw opportunities to tell these sorts of stories in conversations, but, when the moment came, I did not have a story. I realized one day that unless I intentionally collected stories and took care to remember them and craft them into useable forms I would never be able to take advantage of those opportunities. So I began to write stories down. Eventually, I trained my brain to perk up when something occurred that would make for a good story, make a mental note, and tuck it away.

To do this, you must be open. Awake. Not walking around in a way that the world and all its amazing plotlines scroll past without notice. Open your eyes and see the world, see people, and you'll see their stories playing out in front of you. We are conditioned to keep our heads down, stick to our tasks, and do what we do. We have to break out of this and begin to live intentional and fully awake lives.

Collecting stories is not only the end to this sort of life, it is also a means. It is a practice.

You will have to develop a system of collection and storage. I know some people will use programs such as Evernote, while others will use a more traditional paper-filing system. Originally, I would just use a flip notepad in my pocket. No matter what you do, do it consistently and often.

After you have some stories that tell the character and essence of your ministry, begin creating storytellers. These are the people you entrust the stories to and encourage them to tell others. Help them understand that as parents, students, and volunteers in the ministry, they are the translators to the rest of the congregation. They have the power to shape and form the identity of the youth group in the minds of the people of the church.

This is how you spread the seeds of your ministry to keep your own field fertile and productive, but also to inspire other farmers and fields far beyond what you can imagine.

Like the locavore restaurants that have popped up all over the country, you can create great appeal for your kids. Not only will they know it's fresh, but they'll also learn the story of their "food." You can share the stories of the people who grew it and gathered it. You can learn of people in and around your community who delivered the "food" that provides them with sustenance. Ultimately, like locavore restaurant patrons, your kids can know and become a part of the story of their spiritual food.

I am convinced that the *story* part of this method is just as important, if not more so, than the local part. Just like food, ministry does not develop, grow, and flourish in a Styrofoam container wrapped in clear cellophane. It is real, it is local, and it has a story. The ministry and the people who populate it come from somewhere. They have stories and they need to be heard and told.

"Locavore ministry" then, would be ministry that not only knows the value of its people, but it also knows the value of their stories. Jesus understood this well. Jesus did not tell his disciples to go and build a brand. He told them to go and tell their stories, and the stories of others who had experienced God. The entire Bible is a book of stories, a book of stories that were passed down from person to person. When you look for, collect, and tell stories, you are taking part in the ancient tradition through which people of faith tell the stories of how they witnessed the living God in their world—from the miraculous to the mundane.

Go and tell the stories of God's work in your group, and train others to do likewise.

Miracle Grow Is Not So Miraculous

Imagine a youth minister: early forties, excited, passionate, and ready to do all that it would take to grow discipleship and passion in his group.

He and I had been talking for about 45 minutes at this point. He had read several of the latest youth ministry books and was ready to implement many of the ideas found in them in his youth ministry. He had created a sort of Frankenstein's monster of these different youth ministry ideologies and was going to include the best of each in his youth ministry.

One of the techniques he was most excited about was developing a thriving small group ministry. He talked about how the groups would be both onsite and offsite. They would be divided by sex and whether the youth were in middle or high school. He said he wanted to start with four of these groups to begin with, and then develop more as needed. It all sounded really good. The structures, programs, worship plan, and the small groups all sounded like he had not only done his homework but had a plan to implement it.

Then I asked one question.

"So, how many individual kids do you average each week?"
He looked at me and seemed to brace himself. "Eight."

"Eight per small group?" I asked. "That could work as long
as they are all faithful...."

He interrupted, "No, eight total. Eight kids a week. Probably
12–15 active in the entire life of the ministry, but eight kids a
week."

"Oh?" I said a little too shocked and a little too confused.

I didn't want to turn his glorious plan and structure into
a heaping pile of broken dreams. As we continued to discuss
his group with a much more realistic picture, the realization
dawned on him that he was developing a youth ministry for a
large church in southern California, not rural North Carolina.
His thought, which is one I believe many of us have, was if he
treated his youth group like the groups written about in these
books then it would grow to be like one of them.

I asked how he was going to make the small group thing
work and he said, "Well, we don't have any in the senior high
school guys group, but the senior high girls would have three,
the junior high girls would have three and the junior high guys
would have one to two.

"Okay," I said. "You don't need to develop small groups.
Your youth group *is* a small group." I think he was a little hurt
at first, but then I explained, "You are not a youth ministry
that needs to think about small groups the way the books talk
about it. You don't need the structures and the progressive
learning plans, launches, t-shirts, or small-group coordinators.
And never create a small group of only two junior high boys.
Trust me. It is not pretty."

He smiled. He realized was trying to approach his ministry
with a model that was not made for his church.

Many times in our ministries we are convinced "miracle
grow" is what we need. We find ideas on the Internet, on blogs,
in magazines, and in books like this. I am here to propose
something different.

There is no miracle grow, and anything that claims to be is
snake oil. Worse, it's artificial poison. And you're pouring it into
your land. All it produces is false inflation and quick fixes that

leave the soil more barren, stripped, and full of false hope. It creates unrealistic expectations and is built on "Photoshopped" models of youth ministry that have very little basis in reality. While it might work in the short term, the game will eventually catch up with you, the bubble will burst, and you and your youth ministry will be worse for it.

Cultivating for Growth

First, get rid of the idea that you have the same old soil as everyone else. There is no such thing as "just soil."

Often people trying to start a new garden do not get this simple yet profound fact. Soil is a combination of so many different components: sand, clay, rock (igneous, volcanic, and sedimentary), water, chemicals, waste, decomposing material, fungus, roots, and seed—all combined to make this unbelievably diverse substance we call soil.

Certain plants will only grow in certain types of soil. Some soils are rich, aerated, and full of nutrients. These are your groups from healthy churches at a mature yet forward-moving age in their lifecycle. Others have some of the basic building blocks but need some cultivating, some breaking up, some clearing out. You may need to add some compost and work it over time. Then, there are some soils that are too much of one thing. Finally, there are those that have been stripped, over-used, abused, and/or burned. They are depleted of many of the basic components necessary for growth. Obviously, these are not going to produce bumper crops.

We need to do a regular and thorough soil inspection.

Our churches and youth ministries all have a certain kind of soil. It is a combination of elements, influences, and substances that make up the soil of your ministry. In order to be successful in youth ministry in the local church you not only have to know what nutrients your soil has, but, even more, what your soil is lacking.

When you identify what is lacking, then it's time to make a decision: *"Do I use miracle grow, or do I begin the long hard work of soil cultivation?"*

Maybe you're surprised that, in a book called *Organic Student Ministry,* I'm even considering the question of "miracle grow." The reality is, most do choose the former. Let me tell you something: "Miracle grow" can make just about anything grow, just about anywhere. It certainly appears miraculous. The miracle comes to an abrupt halt, however, when we stop supplementing the dead soil with the compound. Miracle grow does not fix the problem long-term; it is a short-term solution with a definite end. Some might ask, "What if the soil is so barren because of so many years of abuse? What about a little to get things going?" I still say it is never a healthy option. I would rather spend a year cultivating the relational soil of the ministry with very little yield than to cover it up and create an artificial and possibly faulty system for the future.

The alternative is not so quick or easy. The alternative is, however, long term, organic, and sustainable.

Cultivating youth ministry is like cultivating the soil of a garden. Until you get in, start digging around, and experiment with the soil, you will have no clue as to the possibilities that lie underneath. You also will have no clue as to what challenges await you.

One of the most common mistakes youth ministers make, whether going into a new church or helping in an existing ministry, is when they believe they have a plan they can implement immediately, without appreciating the soil first. Sure, there are things they can do, systems and structures that can immediately help. But preparing the soil must come first.

You can go in starting to develop a strong relational base by meeting with lots of parents, youth, and volunteers. This is great! It is very important and will help set you up for success. As you form relationships, do so remembering that each conversation and each day is an opportunity to better understand the elements of the history and personality of the ministry. If you do not do this before implementing and introducing change, you will be developing your understanding of the ministry in a vacuum.

Remember that there is not simply one kind of soil, but there are some materials that combine together to produce either a fertile or barren soil for your ministry. Here are a few of the more inhospitable materials.

Anxiety

I find that when I am working with churches one of the primary materials that make up the soil is the highly volatile chemical of anxiety. Anxiety can make rooting difficult in any soil and any type of church. Churches who do not have a strong foundation and a solid identity can find themselves moving from one form of anxiety to the next. Anxiety is a very interesting soil poison. Not only does it contaminate whatever's grown in it, but it can also become more ingrained the longer it is not dealt with. When your ministry is planted in an anxious culture it rarely ever grows deep roots. An anxious culture causes participants and leaders to consistently jump ship and change their programs, trips, and identities at the smallest sign of trouble. Anxiety produces people who do not know their place in, or the identity of, their ministry.

The best way to deal with anxiety is to have a confident leader who chooses to build consensus and then stays the course to implement, evaluate, and adjust along the way as needed for successful change.

If you are dealing with a church that has a history of jumping from one program and philosophy to the next, the best gift you can give it is *consistency*. And as Edwin Friedman writes in his book *The Failure of Nerve*, be a "non-anxious presence."

Sabotage

This stuff is nasty. It is like the crabgrass of youth ministry. It can happen anywhere, and it spreads quickly—especially in unhealthy churches.

There are lots of reasons why sabotage can begin to take root in your ministry, but one thing is consistent: if you do not deal with it, and deal with it quickly, it will take over and ruin the youth ministry.

This cruel and noxious fungus can come in many forms. Here are some of the most common.

The first is from the outside. Sometimes it is a parent who is angry from dealings with the previous youth minister or a previous pastor. Other times it is a volunteer who got their feelings hurt in a transition or did not feel their gifts were being honored. If these problems are dealt with early, and in a way that is full of grace and compassion, the person can become a productive, healthy member of your team again. If not, they can lead to a sabotaging of the ministry.

It comes in many forms: little comments to other parents, an undermining of the small group material, or blatant lies about you or the minister. If this is the type of sabotage you are facing, the answer if easy. You must talk to the person directly—not accusatorily, but making known the ways you believe this person is undercutting the ministry. Always do this with your pastor's knowledge and knowing that it could all be just a misunderstanding or miscommunication. If you deal with the issue directly, you are doing what Jesus recommended (always a good thing) and making clear that sabotage is not a practice you will honor or accept in the ministry.

Remember, there is another saboteur who is much sneakier than any volunteer or parent could ever think about being. This foe will sneak under your radar every time and strike when you least expect it.

You, yourself, can often be your own worst enemy.

I love the scene in *Talladega Nights* in which Reese Bobby, Ricky Bobby's Dad, blows up at the family dinner at Applebee's. As he is walking away, he says, "I don't know what organ or bone people have that makes them act right, but I was born without it. I'm no good."

I have seen ministers over and over again do the youth ministry version of getting thrown out of Applebee's. Some leaders or volunteers become so accustomed to conflict in youth ministry that it, inadvertently, becomes the only climate they know how to function in. I have seen youth ministers take a completely good and functioning ministry and create conflict for little to no reason.

Be aware that this type of sabotage is the hardest to see coming and the most difficult to rid the ministry of. This is so because it is, literally, an inside job. Never believe that all of your motives are pure and true. When something seems self-destructive, pause, ask hard questions of motives, and make sure you take some time.

Never look at yourself in a ministry vacuum. Always ask the tough questions of what else is going on in your life. See what other areas are unhealthy and ask if they are bleeding over into your calling and vocation. Your life does not exist in compartments. Everything is connected and has the opportunity to influence everything else—for good, or for self-defeat.

Too Many Good Ideas

This one is tricky. Is there such a thing as too many good ideas? You had better believe there is! Every idea needs room to be developed, nurtured, and to grow unimpeded. It is not only a problem of space in the ministry when there are too many good ideas, it is also a problem in the lives of the people who are being ministered to. When focus and attention are divided, it can be almost impossible to create consensus around a ministry or opportunity. In the book *Paradox of Choice*, Barry Schwartz outlines the importance of not flooding any marketplace, even the church, with too many choices. Throughout several social experiments the point was proven again and again that the more choices people have the more difficult it is for them to commit to or to pick any option. This plays out in student ministries all over the country each week.

Here is what happens:

We have our baseline ministries: Sunday school, youth group, and maybe some sort of smaller group option. Then one of three things happens: either we see a demographic who is being unreached by our program, we hear about a great new idea at another church or in a book, or a parent brings a "gap" in our programming to our attention. With the best of intentions we seek to create a new ministry opportunity.

Pause.

This is good.

Innovation is productive.

It keeps our ministries relevant, fresh, and moving toward a goal that stands in the perpetual distance.

Innovation is not the enemy.

The problem happens after several years of this sort of activity, when a ministry can and does become bloated by a programmatic overload and this obesity begins to make the ministry both sluggish and cumbersome. I have seen ministry after ministry almost grind to a programmatic halt because of either an overburdened staff or a nonresponsive congregation, made so by a paralysis of choice of ministries.

Again, innovation is not the problem; a lack of pruning is.

A Side Note on Pruning as a Growth Mechanism

Churches are horrible at pruning. Seriously. I mean really bad. Many people become very uneasy when we talk about the church as a business, me too in several instances, but when it comes to pruning we have a lot to learn from the business world. In the business world, if a product or a company is not viable or loses its ability to produce, then it is cut, rebranded, or dissolved. When there is no market for the product, the product stops being produced. This does not happen in churches. We hang onto, pump money into, and keep on life support dying ministries and programs all of the time. Denominations also do this all the time with churches and denominational camps.

I know what many of you are thinking: *I did not get into youth ministry or church work to act like a business,* and I could not agree more. So let me reframe it for you. You and I are caretakers. We are stewards of time, money, emotional bandwidth, spiritual development, and ministerial opportunity for the people who call us their ministers.

That is a hefty job.

One that should not be taken lightly.

If we take this job seriously then we have to, absolutely have to, constantly evaluate and reevaluate our ministries and ministerial priorities to be the most effective they can possibly be. If we are not doing this then we are not being good stewards with the gifts with which God and our people have entrusted us.

Even when I explain this to people, I still I find incredibly well-meaning people asking me the same four questions over and over again. While these have nothing but the best of intentions, they can produce ministry that is ineffective and stifling to all involved.

If It Reaches One Person, Don't We Need to Keep It...?

This type of hardened soil is one of the most frustrating. It's one of the most common phrases I hear when talking about pruning a ministry, the thought that if someone still likes it, we have to keep it. This is faulty reasoning. If we lived in a world that had 80-hour days and where money and time were not restrictive, then we could think about our ministry in these terms. But that is not the world we live in. We have limited resources, time, and abilities. For this reason we have to pick and choose ministries that are more effective than others.

If a ministry reaches only a couple of people, a few questions have to be asked. Why are they attracted to this ministry? What sorts of time and resources is this ministry or program using? Last, and more important sometimes, is this a program that will die out with in a few years on its own? The idea behind this is that some programs have a natural life cycle that pretty much allow them to fade into the background in a couple of years on their own.

For example, I had a ski trip that one group really pushed for when they were in ninth grade, so we did it and it was very popular for around four years, until they graduated. We put the sign-up online their senior year and far fewer people registered than any other year. When we probed the next year to see if it was still viable, the people in the lower grades told us that it was "sort of the graduated seniors thing," and they were interested in this other trip that we were doing instead.

Certain aged youth will often take on a trip or program as their own and will perpetuate it, and often when they leave so does the need for that program. So when you are faced with the, "If it reaches one person...?" question, determine these things:

1. Will it die out on its own? If so, let it.

2. Is it something that is using more time and effort than the yield that it is producing? Provide it with a dignified final run and redirect its few followers into other more life-giving areas of the ministry. (Many times this will come as a relief to them because they have, often times

unknowingly, felt and taken on the burden of keeping it afloat.)

3. Is it beneficial or a crutch for the people involved? Sometimes people will hole themselves away in a program so that they do not have to engage in the larger ministry. This is not always problematic, but can often create a sense of several youth groups and can cause divisiveness in the ministry.

The final word really comes down to, Is it worth the investment? Does it really get us, in the best way possible, to our goals as a ministry? Do not fool yourself, there will always be someone who will come, so do not let that be your criteria. Are lives being challenged, nurtured, and changed, or is it a place where stagnation reigns? When we look at it objectively the best answer is almost always evident.

It Was Started by So and So, So Shouldn't We Continue...?

Often times there can be an emotional/guilt-based attachment to programs and ministries. When a beloved former leader or group member started a ministry (especially if it was successful for a period) we often keep it around a lot longer than it is viable because we feel guilty. The intentions are good: we want to honor that person through his or her work and its viable history. These are good things at their core; however, they can lodge a ministry in the past and keep it looking backward without ever stepping forward. The best way to honor an inspirational leader, or a ministry that was once strong, is not to keep it on life support but to celebrate what it was and let it inspire us to create what it's next incarnation can be.

Don't We Have to Do Something for *This* Group?

Having specialized groups for everyone under the sun is great for Facebook and Tumblr, but not for churches. Let me go ahead and give you permission: *You do not have to reach every demographic in your community, nor are you called to reach every demographic.* Please never make that mistake in your ministry.

If you make it, you will find you and your ministry so diluted that you will end up reaching very few people, if anyone, effectively. Many people will point to Paul's plea/personal call to "be all things to all people so that some might be saved." 1 Cor. 9:22 I do not think that Paul is telling the church to dilute its identity. He was a church planter and, if you read his letters to the churches closely, he focuses on them—dealing with their problems, strengths, and attributes in ways that are appropriate to the church, its personality, and its people. I am not saying that you do not have to go beyond yourself; that is a vital part of our faith. The trick is, however, to know oneself and to know what is beyond oneself as opposed to being in a completely different continent than oneself. I was working with this very highly liturgical Episcopal church a number of years ago and we were talking innovation. One person in the group wanted the church to do this major initiative toward creating a big, "rock and roll" contemporary worship service.

It made no sense for this church.

It was not going beyond itself, it was completely forfeiting itself in favor of something it did not have the DNA to do.

This is one of the main reasons to have a core mission statement that is well thought out and specific enough to exclude. Yes, you heard me right, your mission statement should help you exclude and say no to things that you are not called to do. Know yourself, know your call, and know that God will fill your DNA gaps with other churches, just as God is filling their DNA gaps with you. That is how the body of Christ works; you are just a piece.

Since It Was So Successful Back Then, Shouldn't We Continue…?

Here it is, the number one killer of ministries. In ministry we are often guilty of believing that our ministries should be a constant in an ever-changing world, and that what worked 15, 20 or 50 years ago should work today because it has eternal principles.

God, yes, *God,* has eternal principles, but everything else is up for grabs.

I was working with a church who, 20 years ago, had a stellar youth choir. The youth choir itself was 20 to 25 percent of the congregation, which is crazy. Twenty years ago the youth choir was the standard for success. Then we left the 1990s and it stopped being the big innovative thing that youth groups did. It also happened in this community that the choir program in the school really grew and the kids who had a musical inclination began to express their gifts there more. What was once an incredibly viable and successful ministry was on life support.

I could point to the three or four cultural and environmental indicators as to why that happened and why it was not longer viable nor would it be. To the church, however, none of that mattered. All that mattered was that their understanding and criteria of success depended solely on seeing a large and vibrant youth choir. We have to help congregations reimagine success and what it looks like.

Churches, like people, tell narratives about themselves. These are narratives both of success and of failure. When a narrow narrative becomes ingrained into a culture, it can severely limit the church and cause its understanding and experience of success to suffer dramatically. When the criteria for success is no longer up to date or relevant, the ministry will constantly suffer from not attaining a goal that, in truth, no longer actually exists.

Think about it. Do we judge the success of telecom companies on the number of landlines they have under their label or the number of long distance plans that form those lines? Of course not! While these were major markers of success 25 years ago we know that the market has shifted and these no longer make sense as standards of the industry.

Do not be a landline-based ministry in an age of cell phones and, more importantly, do not let your church judge you on that basis either.

When these four questions or statements are being used to talk about a ministry and its vitality, take them as warning signs that the ministry is in trouble. When you encounter a program that uses one or more of these as crutches, do not try to pump miracle grow formulas into them; rather, objectively evaluate them and make the hard decision to sometimes prune.

Pruning not only removes dead or dying programs from your ministry, it also makes way for new growth and allows fresh ideas to spring up from these dead and dying areas. When your ministry finds itself in times of stagnation and in the need for some sort of "miraculous" cure, know that a little soil cultivation and pruning will do just the trick to get your ministry back on the path to health and productivity.

A Time to Plant and a Time to Harvest

I have often heard youth ministers, pastors, and parents alike talk about how different a sixth grader is from a twelfth grader. They usually do this to talk about the importance of separating grades and high school from middle school ministries. These are important distinctions. Youth are not only in different places of life and maturity but their baseline abilities to receive, process, and act upon new information and experiences changes dramatically over the course of these six or seven years. That, however, is not what this chapter is about.

Super Mario vs. Zelda

I can remember it like it was yesterday. It was Christmas morning, December 25, 1986. I had just turned six years old and I was opening a present that would revolutionize not only my life but the lives of an entire generation. It was a black box with purple highlights; the box read NES: Nintendo Entertainment System. I was hooked from the moment we pulled it from its Styrofoam case. Excitebike, Kung Fu, and Mike Tyson's Punch

Out were some of my favorites. The standard, however, was Super Mario Bros. From the incredibly catchy tune to the myths of being able to get enough of a run to jump the flagpole at the end of each level, it was the game of games.

There was one catch in Mario that none of us really realized at the time. You had to keep going straight. There was no "free roaming," no decisions about where to go; it was a linear romp from level after level, always moving to the next after you finished the prior.

For too long, major youth ministry books and methods approached students in the same way. It was as though they were on some sort of predetermined linear pathway, where each step precluded the next and could be plotted out in a chart. You completed level 1 before you would go to level 2. Usually these "levels" flowed in a sensible-enough pattern.

The student would go on a trip with the group or come to a big reach event.

We get their information and get them to stage 2: youth group.

The funnel continues with Sunday school or the like.

Next, deeper into a small group.

Finally, we hope to get them to the core level of leadership/ service.

It makes sense; well, it *did* make sense.

Fast forward a few months later to Easter morning 1987. I was hooked on Super Mario Bros. Loved it and many other games, nothing could be better; well, that is, until my friend Link came along and changed gaming forever. The Legend of Zelda took an already revolutionary gaming system to an entirely different level. I remember putting the new, beautiful, shiny gold cartridge into my Nintendo and pressing the power button; the waterfall appeared and the music began. I hit the start button and everything changed. I had no clue what to do! Suddenly, I could go anywhere. I could hack down some Q-bert–looking bad guys or chop up a bush. I could cross bridges or go into a cave. I could go almost anywhere; I was free in this virtual world. There was no predetermined path, for the most part. Yes, there were levels and there were objects, once acquired, that would allow me to get other objects, but for the most part I could come and go freely.

Student ministry has become a lot more like the Legend of Zelda and a lot less linear. While we once believed in set entry programs, we are now understanding that students are coming in at all points along the journey. "Missions and service" used to be a sign that a student was committed and core to our ministry; now, it is one of the primary places new and unaffiliated students enter. Small groups are no longer for the older kids who want to go deeper into the Bible. It is a place for community, and students are wanting that much sooner than I have ever seen in my 16 years of ministry experience. The rules of the game have changed, but many of us are still treating students as if they'll accept a linear program, when, in fact, they are already exploring this new, wide-open world that youth ministry must embrace.

Moving from Programs to Practice

I am finding that students' spiritual formation lines are no longer drawn along time spent in the group, decisions made, or age. More and more, I am seeing students plug in where the ministry meets a need that they have. It can be a personal need or the need for a place to express what they are feeling called to do. These needs are not dictated or regulated by any funnel or pathway, but rather by their own personal experiences and life situations. They are real and authentic, and are craving ministry that meets them in those places. When we think about the spiritual development of students, we can no longer understand them as cars being developed on some Henry Ford factory line. Instead of the linear program-based method we were used to, we have to re-imagine students' spiritual development as being open *practice-based*.

Since there seems no observable path, we have to align our programs and ministries with a spectrum of practices that will ensure crucial needs are being met within each planned opportunity. The youth will find the place that feeds them and meets their spiritual needs; we have to make sure that these points are easily accessible and exude the character and DNA of our ministry

The Four Universal Practices

Embrace Hospitality

You cannot do good ministry without hospitality being a core part of its DNA. For so long, hospitality was understood as an "extra," "bonus," or "if we have time" part of a youth group's plan. No longer! Hospitality is an ancient value of Christianity that has regained prominence in the past few years. Books and articles have been written by the truckloads about the practice of hospitality in the church. I believe that nowhere in the realm of Christianity, is hospitality more important than in youth ministry. Youth ministry is not only the most transient ministry but also the most volatile in regards to an experience (what a student's first, second, or third impression is) to return (their likelihood to give it a second, third, or fourth chance) ratio. For this reason, hospitality can no longer primarily operate in our "welcome mat" programs. Long gone are the days when guests came to your student ministry through these designated programs. Almost every time we open the door in our student ministry we are seeing guests walk through. This is not only exciting, it is also daunting.

Keys to Youth Group Hospitality

- **Greet Them**—There has to be someone, someone dedicated and not by chance, at the entrance welcoming them into the area where the youth are gathering or to the event they are attending.

- **Meet Them**—This is the most important step in regard to how we interact with these students in the future. First, introduce yourself to them. Then have them fill out a guest welcome card. This is so important; if you are going to follow up with them, you have to get this information. Last, this is when the student is handed off to another student (one who has been trained in what to do with a guest) to do the rest of the process. You introduce the students and tell the guest that he or she will be with _____ for the rest of the night.

- **Seat Them**—The host students now stays with their particular guests for the rest of the night. They seat them with their friends at the meal or at the event. It is critical that they introduce them to others in their group and help broaden their relational circle.

- **Repeat Them**—This is the final part of the hospitality puzzle. There has to be an invite to the next thing the student ministry is doing, and it needs to come from the guest's host friend. We want "repeat" guests in the student ministry.

Hospitality goes beyond these simple yet important steps. It is a culture shift that your entire group must embrace. You as the leader must not only teach it but constantly model it. Make sure to help students also understand the biblical principle behind it and that it is not a church growth mechanism. This authentic understanding and practice can become ingrained in your youth ministry and flow through every part of it as the first of the four universal practices.

Encourage Belonging/Community

Just beyond out basic needs of food, water, and shelter, there is a primordial need to belong. From the earliest traces of humanity we have seen humans group themselves and form common traits and practices. Humanity has wanted to belong to a group for things such as safety and resource sharing for thousands of years. As belonging evolved, it added another characteristic: the need for community and interpersonal interaction. This need plays out in more prominent ways every day. We see it in every realm—from what team you affiliate with to what GroupMe you are attached to.

This is not to bash the ineffective communities of social media and technology. It is, however, identifying the deep need beyond those social media outlets for deep personal interaction and the desire for a group to call you their own, and vice versa.

In youth ministry, we can never depend on the idea that community happens on its own. It will, as it has for thousands of years, but in youth ministry, more times than not, it must be fostered intentionally and given fertile ground in which to grow.

At one point in our country's history, because of our Puritan origins, religious affiliation was all but a given. With this came a comfortable understanding that churches would continue to have social influence, doctrines ascribed to, and pews filled. We no longer live in that world. Ministers, churches, and religion as a whole carry far less influence than ever before in our country's history. We are no longer a given.

There are far fewer societal standards of which we as a church have tenure. And we must embrace that. When we are no longer in a position of power or privilege, we can truly see and demonstrate what we are made of as a church. We will see what our real beliefs and practices are. There will no longer be any padding of a "social contract" or inherited guilt lining our coffers. We can know beyond the snares of consumerism what our real identity in this world is.

I believe one of the key identifying markers that will distinguish us is a unique form of community.

Please hear me; I believe deeply in teaching and facilitating thoughtful theological reflection and missional living in our students, but neither can happen effectively void of an even deeper sense of community. Please do not hear me say that community is a vessel for these things to happen through, either. Community and belonging are both the means and the ends of any true faith experience. It is both the incubator and the final product. I am convinced that community is more important in youth ministry than ever before. As we move more and more toward being a culture in which religious affiliation does not provide social benefit, the idea of belonging will play a more and more prominent role in our ministries.

Ensure Challenges

As I wrote in my book *Hollow Faith*, the church is not called to be the YMCA. We are called to be a place of belonging, theological reflection, missional living, and communal practice. Challenge is an incredibly important part of this equation. Stanley Hauerwas says in Sunday Asylum: Being the Church in Occupied Territory:

Being a Christian should just scare the hell out of
us. It's like on Sunday we need to rush together for
protection. "Oh, I'm not crazy." That we believe that
God was in Christ reconciling the world is craziness.
It's going to make your life really weird. And you just
need to get together on Sunday to be pulled back into
the reality of God's kingdom.

I not only agree with Dr. Hauerwas, but would push him a
step further: the church should not just be a place where our
people come back to take refuge, it should be so full of crazy
ideas and alternative realities that we become the hub from
which kingdom realities burst forth and find their most fertile
soil.

The short of it is this:

If we are not challenging students in ways that are not only
sometimes illogical but also impractical to their worlds, then
we are not doing our jobs. Belonging is so important because
it provides a safe place to become uncomfortable.

As I write this, I want to make sure that I am very clear that
I am not talking about challenging your students simply to
read the Bible every day or to sign some ridiculous purity cards.
I am talking about challenging them with things that Jesus
actually said, not structures that are born out of our puritan
guilt factories. I am talking about challenging them to read the
Sermon on the Mount and take it seriously. To actually love
an enemy. To trust that God loves you more than a bird of the
field, and to live a life that is not for yourself.

The challenges of purity cards, daily devotionals, and raising
your hands in worship pale in comparison to the kingdom life
that Jesus calls us to. When we set these as the bar, our students
will not only hold them as idols but they will become bored
with a faith that is so easy to attain and master that they are
proficient at it by their junior year in high school. It's no wonder
that, by the thousands, our students are leaving the faith they
grew up with every day.

If a student, with a little self-discipline and perseverance,
can follow closely and live out the faith we are teaching, then
we might want to rethink the gospel we are doling out. I bet
if we look closely we will realize it is full of a lot of rules for

being kind, rubrics for personal piety, and dull self-help religion that would have a hard time cutting through a stick of room-temperature butter.

That is a faith they will leave in a heartbeat once they are out of high school, and for good reason. The problem is that they might go the rest of their lives believing it to be the Christianity that was of Christ instead of a diluted sugary brand of faith-lite that we have become so accustomed to.

Be the difference; challenge them, push them, and do so with the word of Christ, not the cultural expectations of Hallmark cards.

Express Expectation

The final universal practice is the practice of expectation. The first three were practices that came from us as their leaders. They were good, but ultimately were facilitated from within the ranks of the leadership of the ministry. Expectation is different. One of the most important things that we can do in our youth ministries is to expect service, leadership, creativity, and more from our youth. The current expectation of youth ministry is purely consumer in its nature. We work hard to get them into our stores, to browse our aisles, to have brand loyalty and to become repeat shoppers. When we treat ministry like this, we will not only lose our identity as the church but we will also always be judged on customer satisfaction ratings and growth dividends. Sound familiar? Like, maybe, the last few meetings you had with parents or your senior pastor?

I am convinced that the only way to get beyond these consumerist tendencies is to refuse to play by those rules. Okay, now let me pause and clarify a few things:

What I have just said is in *no* way an excuse to:

Communicate poorly
Not listen to your students and parents
Lead sloppy ministry
Be lazy
Fail to think and practice creativity in how you market (technical way of saying how you talk about and tell the narrative of) your ministry

The soapbox is one you have heard and repeated several times. We expect our youth to attend football practice, go to piano rehearsal, do their homework, and everything else under the sun that they have committed to. We have to move out of, and help our families move out of, the mindset that our faith does not have expectations as well. If we do not have expectations we have told our students that it is not as important as the things that we do have expectations for.

Plain and simple.

When we have expectations for something, we place an automatic value on whatever that is, a value that is not placed on things that we do not hold the same expectation of.

Expectation tells our students that they have a role in this, and it is not just for them. Expectation tells them that what we are doing is important and that it is important enough to take priority. And this goes not only for parents as well—it goes for you too. As youth ministers we have to expect our students to co-minister in the ministry with us. If we are always the ones who lead, teach, pray, read, plan, etc., then we never give them the ability to buy in and to practice alongside people who already know how to do these things.

If we want to engage our students where they are, we have to know that a part of that is to expect something from them. Expectation goes back to that primordial idea of belonging as well. You know you belong to a group or a community when there are expectations on you, when you have a job and have responsibilities. We have to re-imagine the idea of expectation in the church. Too often we talk about it like expectation is equal to a burden. When we practice expectation well, it becomes a means to belonging, to being depended on and having ownership.

When we are practicing these four principles, we know that our ministries will have places for students to be ministered to and to minister with, no matter where they are in their journeys. Without using the false pretenses of age and linearly prescribed paths, we also allow our students to move about freely, without unnecessary roadblocks within our ministries. When we saturate all of our programs with *Hospitality,*

Belonging, Challenge, and *Expectation,* we will find that they are all conducive environments for first timers, veterans, and everyone in between.

It is not that our programs lose their distinctive qualities (small groups provide more intimate times, and youth group might have more games), it just means that we re-imagine the ways our programs interact with each other and lead to our students progression into a deeper discipleship.

6

Cage-Free Mission

Do you remember?
Do you remember being a youth?
I do.
Do you remember what you learned in youth group? Maybe.
Do you remember what you did at youth group? Probably more so than what you learned.

Do you remember being impassioned, excited, completely enthralled in the urgency of whatever your youth group was selling as the dire need of the world at that moment? Do you remember when the entire existence of heaven, hell, and the known world depended on that mission trip, that outreach night, or that drive to help children in Africa?

I do, and I would guess that those are the very things we remember most. As youth ministers, we know that those are our glory moments, those are the moments we live for. Those are the moments when we know that fringe youth are getting it, or see that a youth leader come into his or her own. Those are our "money" moments.

But could it be that those moments—the ones we glory in the most—might be some of the most detrimental to our students?

Now, don't get me wrong. Those times are magical. Those times are often when God is speaking most clearly to our students, the moments are not the problem. It's every moment after where we find ourselves in trouble.

Most of us are good at getting people wrapped up in something; most of us have some charismatic quality that allows us to do these things. That is part of our gifting. The problem is that the church, and especially the part of the church responsible for students, has often been incredibly irresponsible with the passion of its young people.

Passion is the currency that paves the roads to the kingdom of God. Passion—deep, imitate, youthful passion—has funded everything from national revolutions to the civil rights movement. Passion is valuable, even precious.

We may be great at doing drives and fundraisers that bring great manifestations of passion, but we can also be guilty of a poor investment strategy. In theory, we care greatly about the treasure of this passion, but, in practice, we squander it like a prodigal.

We bring the passions of the youth to a great and beautiful crescendo through our teaching, slide shows, statistics, short-term missions, and worship, only to stop the symphony short and take the rest of the music home with us. We guide them to the runway and we never give them the opportunity to fly.

One of the greatest sins of the church is telling the youth they have to change the world and then failing to give them the space and permission to do so.

Short-Term Shortcoming

I know that many of you may have already taken offense just by reading the title, "Short-Term Shortcoming." And, in all truthfulness, I do too. I do because of the amazing things I've seen accomplished in short-term mission situations. Amazing things happen—both among those serving and those receiving. In truth, most of the time the lines between those who are supposed to be the givers and those who are supposed to be the receivers becomes so blurred that everyone ends up on the receiving end in some way.

So far, so good. But too often this is what the youth (and consequently the church) eventually come to believe that being "on mission" means. However, because these trips are "done" for the youth, it is so easy for them to fall into the trap of going on missions instead of understanding their lives as their mission. What is the old saying about teaching someone how to fish?

Again, please understand me. There is nothing wrong with mission trips. The problem comes when we begin to see a "trip" as the pinnacle of our thinking and action.

What if we understood the trip as only one cog in a larger process of our life as mission? What would happen if we let that new perspective shape our student ministry?

I suggest that great things begin to happen! But these great things will bring with them new problems of their own—problems such as not having enough stuff for some zealous passionate teenagers to do.

Our natural response to enthusiastic students is to start their new initiative for them. However, with this approach, sooner or later we will find ourselves going to the food bank with a different group of kids ten times a week. There's a better idea.

What if instead of the student minister finding and facilitating the ministry opportunities for the students, the students found and facilitated the opportunities for us? Ministerial suicide? I don't think so. With the right parameters, this shift could be one of the best moves we ever make.

Just imagine the looks on the parents' faces when their teenagers are suddenly heading up one of the church's outreach ministries to homeless men or battered women in your area? Can you even imagine the look a parent will give when an eighth-grade son asks for help in finding some statistics on local poverty levels in your area?

Imagine no longer.

Students without Walls

I am not suggesting we give the students a $10,000 budget and tell them to plan a trip to Africa. Actually, it is just the opposite. Remember...think organic. Think homegrown.

Think about utilizing and giving legs to that amazing youthful passion.

Our job is to allow our students—better yet, *enable* our students—to take hold of their passions, learn about them, and then develop an action plan to make a difference in their world and community. I have to give fair warning, though. This sort of unleashing of passion for mission projects that actually launch will not just happen. Our students will need our help with goal setting, oversight, and coaching, but those steps are part of the fun.

Remember, the goal is not to get youth to go on a mission trip; it is to enable them to begin to live missional lives—and to live so missionally that others are introduced to the missional lifestyle as well.

This process releases the students from waiting until the summer to satisfy their missional hunger. We free them to no longer be dependent on the student ministry to do what Jesus called us all to do. Ultimately we free them to become more fully Christian.

Sara's Story

"Hey Stephen, I really want to do an ice cream social for old people and poor people." "Why?" I asked. "Because those are some of the saddest people I see and I just figured ice cream makes everyone a little happier."

I thought to myself, "Hmmm...Sara is a really sweet girl, maybe a little idealistic, but really sweet."

"How do you intend on doing this, getting the word out, and just logistically making this happen"? I asked.

To my surprise, she had already figured out where to get plenty of ice cream donated. She had identified some organizations that would bring the elderly. And she had actually already begun working with our county chamber of commerce to come up with a list of those who would qualify as "the poor."

Sara had a mission. She had a plan. All she needed was a little permission (which I was more than happy to give!).

What if this story was not the exception but the norm? What if student initiatives like this became normal, everyday occurrences in our student ministries? It can and should be.

Sara had something most of our students do not know they have permission to have. She had initiative. Many of our students see the student ministry as a place to go and be observers and participants. They have become victims of a culture that views leadership as an almost exclusively upfront experience.

In most student ministries, the students themselves are rarely up front and so they rarely feel empowered to take real leadership. I know, I know. Many of our students are "called" leaders. Heck, many of them are even elected as leaders, but few ever really get the chance to lead in way that is not puppet-mastered by the youth minister or the church.

The "Runaway Youth" Syndrome

One of best things about this understanding of mission is that it is not limited by the youth minister's knowledge, experience, or passions. Too many times student ministries take on only the personality of the youth minister who is leading them at that particular time. Our youth ministries become just a little bit like Julia Roberts' character in *Runaway Bride*.

Let me explain. Remember how every time she began to date a guy, her entire identity would begin to meld into whatever passions, interests, and beliefs the guy had? She would duck out of the relationship at the last minute, because something deep within her knew she would lose her identity in the process.

How many times does this happen to our groups? You might never notice it, but I am certain our churches do. A new, young, energetic youth minister comes in with passions for working with those who are mentally challenged. Then, suddenly, many of the programs, missions, and activities are focused around that priority.

As the group begins to get passionate about that topic and rally around it, are they rallying around the mission or around the youth minister? After a few years, this youth worker leaves, and the group shifts its identity again.

While it is good and necessary to expose the youth to new missions and passions, too often a group (and a leader) can get tunnel vision, leaving many of the most obvious missions by the wayside.

It's the runaway bride syndrome all over again, co-opting the missional identity of their leader, rather than being invited to discover their own. The movie takes a turn when the main character is finally "given permission" to be who she is. She is told she has to stop taking on the loves and interests of her boyfriends and discover her own. And after she finds "herself," she discovers fulfillment not in the passions of others but in her own. What if we were in the business of helping youth find themselves, their passions, and their interests, and of giving them permission to live this out, supported by the student ministry?

Action Teams

I began to imagine how we might make this shift in thinking just a natural part of our youth ministry, and I began to experiment with an idea that has come to be known as "Action Teams."

One night at youth group, I gave a message about embracing our unique passions for mission. I pitched the idea of Action Teams, explaining that these would be groups of 5–10 youth who would come together under the banner of a similar passion.

I encouraged anyone interested to come by later that week with the names of the people they'd like to have on their team, and I promised to help them each develop action plans for their passions. My guess was, if the results were like what happens after most of my messages, there would be one or two small teams who would come by that week or maybe even the next.

What happened shocked me.

Ten minutes after my message, I had five action teams wanting to schedule a meeting with me to discuss how they could change the world. It was awesome.

The passions ranged from topics such as AIDS in Sub Saharan Africa to Clean Water Needs to helping people cope with depression. Students were bringing things I had not even thought about, things I was not remotely educated in. And that was the point. They were about to take *me* on a mission.

Letting Youth Take You on a Mission

I knew I had to get a lot more serious if I didn't want to miss this amazing opportunity. The next morning I came in to work and developed a rubric for how to empower and enable the youth to successfully *learn, teach, act,* and *impact* their missional passion.

Learn

The easy thing to do was to tell my students to go and find an organization to plug their energy into. The better road, I believe, was to give them information to help them begin their work. They were not looking to the youth ministry to pick them up and drop them off at the "result." They wanted to work, feel, and maneuver their way to their own destinations.

So I took a list of their ideas and gave an hour of time to developing a base of resources and websites for them to educate themselves with. After making this list I gave it to each of them and sent them off with two things: (1) a challenge to learn all they could about the subject, the reasons it's a problem, and how others are working to solve it, and (2) a mandate to complete their research in two weeks, so that, two weeks from that time, they could come and teach me all they had learned.

Teach

Once the two weeks had passed, the next step was to help the youth be able to interpret, translate, and teach their findings to others. We challenged them to spread the word about their passion, which almost always came as a natural spilling over of their passionate involvement with the subject matter. During the two-weeks-later meeting and subsequent meetings (if more problems arose and needed to be researched), I hoped to see a few things happen. Sometimes a full discussion of the research required a little prodding on my part. But asking tough questions and helping with problem solving was just a part of the process.

Every student was challenged with the question, "How can you effectively tell others what you have learned?" And, together, we would develop a plan to share the discoveries to see if there might be others interested in joining the Action Team as well.

We ended up establishing a mission moment each week or month during the main youth gathering, a time when our action teams were given the floor, armed with handouts and multimedia capabilities to educate their friends and leaders about their action plan.

The beautiful thing to watch was the growing missional culture and buzz that was beginning to bubble up in our group. More and more, their missional awareness revolved around "everydayness," no longer limited to a trip that happened once a year in the summer.

Act

After awareness was raised within the group and new people added to particular Action Teams, it was time to cut them loose. This can come in a variety of ways. One great way is to raise awareness throughout the rest of the congregation. We asked our senior pastor if, once a month, a different team could give their presentation during Sunday morning worship services, in hopes that adults might hear and choose to join one of these Action Teams.

Another initiative involved simple fundraisers as a part of an awareness campaign. Some youth developed letter-writing partnerships with a locality, through which the youth wrote letters of encouragement to the people affected by a disaster. Others wrote letters to their senators and congressmen to advocate for a just cause. We realized that the possibilities are really limitless!

Impact

The last cog in the plan, after campaign and action have been taken, is to help give sustainability. Most of my experiences with these Action Teams focus around missional opportunities that are overseas. This is good. And I don't want to do anything to discourage it.

But it is important and necessary for the youth to understand that, while Jesus called us to "go to the ends of the earth," he also spent most of his ministry helping those who he came across on a daily basis. In an effort to encourage our youth's overseas missions and, at the same time, help them see needs all around them nearby, we developed the concept of Mirror Missions.

A mirror mission, as its name suggests, is a local missional opportunity that mirrors in some way a global missional focus—finding a local expression of a global need. A focus on AIDS in Africa could be mirrored through involvement with the local AIDS coalition in your area. Hunger in Haiti could mirror work with a local food bank or kitchen.

After you and the team decide on what the local mirror is, you repeat the *learn, teach,* and *act* steps all over again for that local systemic problem. When you get to the impact step, you are developing a hands-on plan to help with that cause in your own community, without abandoning the global arm of your students' passions.

Action Summit

We have found it helpful to think of the Action Team process in a cycle of around nine months. Action Teams are not broken up or abandoned at the end of nine months. But new Action Teams are allowed and encouraged to launch once a new cycle has begun. It is valuable to allow projects to have a clear "end point" to allow youth the freedom to explore new initiatives in the next cycle.

Having a set end to a cycle gives the group, congregation, and even the community an opportunity to celebrate these students and their work. We call this our Action Summit. We make it a great festival, held in the fellowship hall or on the church grounds, showcasing each team's cause, and sometimes matching a food festival to match each country being served. It's even possible to make this event an additional churchwide fundraiser, giving congregants the chance to pay an "admission" to come walk around, sample the food, and view booths set up by the youth about their Action Team's focus.

In addition, we love to provide each team with time to showcase their individual campaign efforts and tell the stories of their mirror mission. The funds raised can be sent to different organizations represented or even be put back into a special account to fund the next cycle of Action Teams.

Amazing things can and will happen when we uncage our youth, encourage and empower them, and ultimately allow them to take us on mission!

Remember Sara?

So Sara had her ice cream social; in fact, she had four of them! They did exactly what she wanted them to do. These events brought people who were generally lonely and sad and it gave them a time for community, fun, and a little piece of happiness. It was incredible; she took me and our church on a mission. You have the chance for your youth to take you on a mission too!

7

Harvest Feasts, Christmas, and Constantine

Constantine may seem like a strange figure to mention when talking about organic student ministry. After all, student ministry did not really exist until around 1600 years after Constantine.

Despite this fact, Emperor Constantine can teach us something very useful when we begin to think about what our year and years in student ministry look like.

We are, in many ways, tasked like Constantine to create a calendar by which to help our youth understand and practice their faith throughout the year.

Already I am hearing my Episcopal brothers and sisters whispering in my ear, "What about the Lectionary? Don't forget the Lectionary." I cannot but agree with the ghosts of Anglicans past as they urge me toward an established and well-worked guide to finding the significance in our Christian year.

As a matter of fact, if you are Anglican or have already fully incorporated the Lectionary into your student ministry, with important dates and celebrations marked, then feel free to skip this chapter.

If, however, you are the sort of youth minister who struggles to plan series for your youth when it isn't Christmas or Easter, or you've ever just remembered Lenten pledge cards on the morning of Ash Wednesday, then keep reading.

All I Want for Christmas Is a Blood Ritual?

First, let's back up to the mid fourth century. Constantine has had a conversion experience, but is faced with a dilemma. You see, Constantine was involved in a very pluralistic society—in fact, maybe one of the most pluralistic ones the world has ever seen. He knew, wisely, I think, that to just take all of the established holidays, feasts, and festivals and try to stop them and add a new "Christian" calendar with new holidays and feasts on new days was political suicide—not to mention the fact that it would insight massive revolts against Christianity.

He decided to start with the beginning of Jesus' life and let that be the first Christian holiday incorporated into the fabric of his society. As he took in the scope and range of what was happening in the calendared year, he found the festival commemorating the birth of Mithras, the Persian god of light. This festival began on December 25 and lasted through January 1. He was smart; it is not like he decided to make Christmas happen on March 22, which just happens to be the festival of Die Sanguinas, or the day of blood. Wouldn't it be a great Christmas celebration, getting up early in the morning and running down stairs so that the family could practice a ritualistic bleeding ceremony together before going down to the church where the priests would castrate themselves in honor of the holiday?

No, Constantine decided to choose a holiday that corresponded better with the story of the nativity, and put at the center elements of the birth of Christ. From its beginning, Christmas was a holiday in which gifts were exchanged, families and friends gathered to feast, and a birth was celebrated—just like in the Roman and Persian festivities. What if we examined the modern Western calendar, found those naturally occurring shifts and pauses in the year of the country, state, community, school, and church? As we examine these already embedded ebbs and flows in the year, we can take them and filter through to find the ones that seem to naturally fit and even compliment the Christianity we are trying to link to and instill in the students.

Why More Holidays?

Why would we celebrate more holidays? Do we not complain that (1) there are too many holidays to contend with, and (2) they have become so commercialized that they have lost their true meanings anyway? YES and YES! These are some of the exact reasons why we should begin to think about our youth ministry calendars in this very way. Countless sociological studies have shown the importance of ritual and rhythm in the life of a religious youth. Christian Smith's *Soul Searching*, a study of the American teenager, showed that students involved in religious communities with much ritual and rhythm are some of the most likely to live lives in which that religion has a continual influence into their adulthood. So much of a teenager's life is full of inconsistency and a very short-sighted understanding of his or her situations and conflicts. And, if we are being honest, some of these statements apply to many of our adults and even our clergy!

One great way to combat this is to order our year around a calendar in which we no longer accept Thanksgiving as the beginning of the shopping season, but rather begin to redefine these celebrations, recover their original meanings, and, in some cases, co-opt new, more Christian meanings. One of the religions that best exemplifies living with the stories and values of one's faith at the core of the calendar is that of our Jewish brothers and sisters.

Judaism has 12 main feasts and festivals. They are wonderfully arranged and tell the story of the Jewish people's faith. One might say that one of the best ways practicing Jews could explain their faith and their faith's story is to hand outsiders their PDAs. If you have never studied these feasts and festivals, I would encourage you to take the time to go and talk to a rabbi or a Jewish friend and learn about the Jewish calendar and the significance of each of their holidays. If you are able to attend some of these celebrations, you will notice that they are multigenerational, lively, and, most of all, riddled with meaning and story.

So, I am not suggesting we add a lot of new holidays to our calendar, but what if we took a meaningful look at the things that are already on our calendar? What if we really examined those natural things that happen throughout the year, those natural times of starting and stopping, times of death and birth, and times of joy and celebration?

How to Avoid Reinventing Lent

In doing this, one of the best things we can do is to begin at the beginning. There are some *great* resources out there that will help mark your and your students' years in significant and Christian ways. This is a point at which I will default back to our Episcopal friends. If you are not familiar with the *Book of Common Prayer,* get familiar! Find your friendly neighborhood Episcopalian and ask him or her to give you the short and skinny on this wonderful book, which is full of rituals and means of celebration. Learn the ins and outs of this resource and begin to understand the depth and consistency such a resource can bring.

The Christian liturgical calendar is also a great resource you can download online, and there are even some versions you can put directly on your digital calendar. The other base resource I would highly recommend looking at is a calendar that has a complete listing of the feast days of the saints. I know for some there will be an initial pushback on this, because of the title "saint." I would encourage you to not let this gut reaction deter you from checking out this invaluable resource and allowing the stories and lives of some of the faith's most amazing lives to teach our youth and us.

The Episcopalians have done us a great service in developing a list of saints who are not included on the traditional list provided by the Roman Catholic Church. These include Martin Luther King Jr. and Gandhi. Such calendars are great tools to begin learning about how history has been celebrated in the Christian Church throughout its existence. As you study, mark some saints and observances that seem to correspond with themes familiar to you as you think about things that are significant in your culture, community, and church.

Celebrating Significance

Now that we have established that we do not need to reinvent the wheel in terms of established holy days, we can move on to discovering new celebratory times in our student ministry. This is one of the most fun parts in this whole process. Some keys to success in doing this are not to rush it, and to keep our ears to the ground. When I say do not rush this process, I really do mean it. This process should at the very least take a year of paying attention, noticing seasonal shifts, taking note of missed opportunities to mark significant events, and then finally determining what best complements what already naturally occurs in the calendar.

It is important to remember that doing this is not about imposing "more" or "adding" significant events. What it is about is highlighting and taking time to bring attention to events that are already in the life of the ministry, students, or community. Before thinking about what these are, I think it is important to revisit the Jewish feast days. Not all of the holidays and festivals are riddled with joy and good feeling. It is just as important to mark and recognize those times in the life of the community that have been marked by tragedy and loss. Again, think about what is already happening in the minds and hearts of the students, recognizing and validating those feelings. An example of this would be if there has been the loss of a member of the student ministry. What better way to honor that memory as well as doing an excellent pastoral care piece than to embrace that loss on it's first, second, and third anniversary? Eventually the hurt will fade to the background and, while most of the pastoral care work is finished, you have a new opportunity. That new tradition can then be morphed into a remembrance of all who were lost in that past year among the group's families, friends, and community.

With the understanding that not all events need be celebratory out of the way, let's focus on two possible times in the year whose significance can be celebrated. The first that comes to mind is actually the day after I am penning these words. Earth Day is April 22 each year and is celebrated in many places—church not always being one of them. I have found that at a time when we are so inundated with negative news about our world, it is important to celebrate the positive. Earth Day, while relatively unknown several years ago, is now a nationally recognized day to promote the well being of our home, God's creation. I believe this is a wonderful time to do a couple of things that will solidify this part of the year as a time to think about creation and our stewardship of it.

One way to highlight this day is to have the students read and reflect on a different day of the creation story each day of the week leading up to April 22. Another way is to plan a ministry-wide clean up of a local green area. If you are wanting to add a more significant service piece to your body of service opportunities for the year, you could use this as a launch for an adopt-a-mile initiative for the student ministry. We did this at a church in which I served. It was relatively simple, but made a difference in the lives of the students, as well as the mile and a half we were responsible for cleaning up every three months. While some will argue that Earth Day does not have much religious significance, I would argue that it is all about how you interpret or, in some cases, reinterpret it.

Another idea has more to do with the changing seasons and, in particularly, the shortest day of the year. I happen to know exactly when the winter solstice is because it is the day before my birthday. December 21 has been referred to as the shortest day of the year, which in turn also makes it the longest night of the year. While living in Atlanta, I was introduced to the idea of doing an event that empathized with the homeless on this cold and longest night of the year. This could translate into a number of activities. The first could be to actually do a sleep in at a local park with other groups to bring local and media attention to the longest night of the year and your community's homeless population. While this would work for some groups, it is not for everyone. For those of you who might find yourselves jobless after such an event, you could take a more tame but just as effective approach.

Many groups participate in a "relay for life," in which sponsors pledge a certain amount of money to cancer research per lap a youth completes. You could take this same concept and set it up so people could pledge money to a homeless ministry for the number of hours a youth slept outside on this longest night of the year. If the youth group buys into this, the possibilities are endless to the amount of awareness and funds that can be raised by essentially doing a really well-insulated camp out. Again, these are just a few ways to take naturally occurring events and showcase their significance both spiritually and socially.

School Rules! No, Seriously, It Does

Now that we have come up with some really interesting and significant events, we have to ask ourselves: "How does this fit into my non-negotiable calendar?" When it comes down to it, if we are being honest with ourselves the thing that rules the lives of our students more than any other outside force is school. It determines how students and families live, work, shop, play, vacation, eat, sleep, celebrate, and sometimes even fight! For 12 years of their lives (sometimes even more) the school and subsequent school activity calendar determine the ebb and flow of the family's year. I have been more frustrated and have beat my head on many a wall because I forgot to consult the almighty school calendar before planning an otherwise awesome retreat, small group, or event. Nine week's tests, finals, and school holidays can make or break some major events and some hard work put into your student ministry.

There are two ways to approach the school calendar, and I believe both are needed to tap into the rhythms of your students lives. Now, remember that neither of these ideas are profound in theory, but in practice, which most student ministries do not do, they are invaluable. The first is to go though the calendar when it is published—most schools have these on their websites three months before the year begins— and mark your "red flag" days and weekends. These are the times in the year that you should avoid having any sort of retreat or off-site event. In some cases, it is even prudent to not schedule your regular programming. We have found in our student ministry it is important to not plan retreats during the times of major testing in our school system.

We accidentally did this for one of our major junior high retreats and lost one third of our students for the retreat. Another consideration to take into account are those three- and four-day weekends. You will have to make those decisions based on the trends on your community. In our church, Labor Day weekend is out, but we always take a really successful, fun retreat on Martin Luther King weekend.

Again, it is important to observe, ask, and note the trends in your particular community and then make your plans. If you are able to discover one of those long weekends during which the students tend to not vacation, and can establish an effective retreat, your student ministry will own that weekend from that point on. This is a great way to lock in your students and community students into a sense of expectancy for that weekend every year.

Just a side note on this: if your community is like mine, there are churches that have already figured the whole "locking in a certain weekend" model. If this is the case, it is important to "red flag" these weekends as well, especially if there is a community draw to the event.

The second red flag technique is to note when significant things are happening, such as finals and large school-wide functions, plays, relay for life, festivals, etc. Unlike above you are looking for the weekends and weeks when you need to reconsider your regular weekly programming. This will also enable you to plan your year and weeks with those events in mind so you can make sure to support the youth in their realm. This is especially good for finals time, when the student ministry has the opportunity to provide a much-needed study break for the youth, full of snacks, coffee-style drinks, and a relaxing activity or two. Again, this in not rocket science, but it is amazing how poorly we all tend to look ahead in the calendar and really adopt the school calendar as our own.

Throughout all of this calendar preparation, it is important to remember the big picture. No matter how much fun doing an Earth Day worship service is, or how meaningful a longest night of the year mission project might be, the whole reason to do this is *rhythm*. It is about learning the rhythms of the students' lives—having the ability to move with them and giving the student ministry the ability to be prophetic by making meaning inside of them. It also means helping students see time and holidays in a very different way. It calls us to see our moments as God's moments, and to note that, whether it is Valentine's Day or day set aside for remembering a tragedy, our God is with us just the same.

8

Ebb and Flow

For years I found myself going into a pretty bad depression each year during the months of February and March. It was tough. For some time I chalked it up to the winter blues and all of the things that come from a post-holiday hangover. While I processed this as the answer verbally, in the back of my mind I knew that there was something more, something that was just out of my reach. I came home from church one Wednesday night in late February and I was ready to quit. I was so tired of feeling like a failure, so tired of feeling rejected and so…just… *tired*. My wife asked how church went that night; I said it was horrible. She asked why, and I told her that I just felt like no one was there. Then she said something that changed my whole perspective. "Stephen, you get like this every year around this time. You know that just because they are not there does not mean that they are rejecting you; you should not take it so personally." Then it hit me.

She is right; I do take it really personally. She was also right that I get down at around this time every year. When I put the two together, I realized something that has helped ease and eliminate anxiety every since. There are just some times of the year when attendance is going to be down, no matter what we do. I know this is not rocket science, but it is certainly profound for how we look at and understand the nature of the ministries that we run.

I was not only failing to keep track of my youth attendance regularly, I was also failing to look for patterns in my ministry. The main problem was that I was not understanding the ministry as the living organism that it is.

Oh, I Love the Beach

As I write this chapter, I am sitting on a screened in deck overlooking a beautiful white sand beach. Jealous, aren't you? You should be. It is beautiful.

My favorite part of the beach is listening to the water. Waves crashing, the recess of the water back into itself—plus the sound of a cool breeze ruffling the palm trees that surround the porch.

Beautiful. I do find it ironic that I just happen to be writing this chapter while I am at the beach. The entire concept for the title of this chapter is based on a phenomenon that occurs on shorelines. If you have spent any time near the ocean, you know that there is high tide and there is low tide. The earth, gravity, the pull of the moon, and a lot of other things I cannot explain combine to create this nautical cycle. One day, my little boy asked me which I like better: the high tide or the low? As I thought about it, I could not decide. So, I told him they were both awesome for different reasons. I like high tide because the water gets deeper, and deeper water means that I get to snorkel more. Also, in high tide you see more fish and have a lot of waves, which is awesome for body surfing. But, on the other hand, when the tide is out there is a whole other part of the beach and ocean you get to see. Usually when the tide is in you focus on the awesome nature of the water. When it is out, you get to see the sand and all of its treasures in a whole other way.

The beach also looks completely different. I remember being in Iona, Scotland, a few years back and walking around that amazing island during low tide. It was incredible how a whole other world came to life when the water was out. It was almost like there were two completely different beaches.

So, Patrick, the answer is: "I like the beach, no matter high or low tide; it is all pretty incredible."

Good Youth Ministry during High and Low Tides

Pause, pump the brakes. Before we can talk about how to do good youth ministry during the high and low tides, we first have to be aware of when those times will occur *before* we are in them! The only way you are going to know this is by doing the hard and diligent work of attendance tracking and calendaring.

This was the first thing my friend and mentor Mark Devries taught me. He has this great spiel (that I often hijack and use myself) about numbers. He will start by talking about being accused by some parents at one point in his ministry that he cared about numbers too much. He goes on to say, "You had better believe that I care about numbers. I look at numbers all of the time. I think about numbers all of the time and I am always concerning myself with numbers." Then he goes on, "Jesus cared about numbers too." Then, in his big-smile, squinting-eyes way, he would trap you: "Remember the 99? He counted them and that is how he knew that one was missing. If Jesus were not concerned about numbers, why was he counting?

"Jesus was counting because each number is connected to a person. Each number we count in youth ministry is connected to a kid." Then he closes the deal on you: "So, you better believe I care about numbers; I care about numbers because I care about kids."

So I tell you now, you had better care about numbers! Don't do the false humility thing. They are your sheep; you had better be a good shepherd! They are important. It took me a while to realize how important attendance tracking really is in order to do good ministry. So for every event, prayer group, mission project, trip, etc., you had better be counting and taking down the name of each student there. At that point, you then have to put them into some sort of system that will allow you to look at them from an organized, objective standpoint.

If you do not have much of a budget to spend on that, Google Docs is a great way to keep up with your information. If you do have a budget to spend on it, I highly recommend Ministry Tracker. However, no matter what you use, it will only be as good as you are about getting all of the data in consistently, and with uniformity. Remember, you need not only to get head counts but have *everyone* sign in as well.

Predicting the Tide

Once you have collected a year's worth of data, you are now set to begin looking for trends and observing the ebb and flow of your ministry—the seasonal changes. Most of the time, this ebb and flow can be directly correlated to one or more calendars. For my context, it involves the high school sports and academic calendars, and the college football schedule. We know at our church that, when Alabama or Auburn has a home night game, we will not see a certain demographic of our people on Sunday morning. They will have been at the game late, and often will not make it to church on Sunday morning. No judgment; it just is what it is. The point is, do not look at the 52 weeks of data in a vacuum, but rather make sure to overlay it with the schedules of the people of your congregation. A few things to notice:

- When are the spikes in attendance?
  - We usually see these in the beginning of the year, after New Years and in April
- When are the troughs?
  - We usually see these around mid-terms, finals, long weekends, dances, and sports seasons— when a large number of our kids are involved.
- When are the anomaly days—either high or low?
  - We usually see high days on Easter, Christmas, Confirmation welcome day.

— We usually see lower days on either side of
Thanksgiving and either side of the Fourth of
July.

Note these observations and watch for them each year. This
will not only be important to help you become less anxious
but it will help you plan for the different seasons of your
community's year.

When to Surf and When to Search for Shells

As the tide changes, so should your ministry. I am not talking
about taking on a radically different approach to ministry or
defaulting on your DNA during transitions. Nuancing your
ministry during these times is wildly important—not as a
reaction but as a way of best ministering to the type of crowd
you have. Back to the beach. Tide was out and my little boy and
I were chest deep in the water, waiting for a wave for him to
body surf into the shore on. We waited and waited and waited.
Finally, he made the astute observation that we were going to
be out there for a long time, and that we should just swim in
and enjoy playing in the sand because the beach was so much
bigger. He was right; we were missing a great opportunity to
play in the sand and look for sand dollars, which were much
more readily available with the tide out.

In ministry, on the other hand, when you are experiencing
high tides you have some opportunities to do things that you
otherwise are not able to do during the majority of the year.
These are great times to do big events, retreats, and trips.
These are also times to really make sure that your hospitality
is firing on all cylinders. The reason why attendance is higher
is because guests and students who are not regulars are visiting
and checking the ministry out. During these exploratory
times, you have a distinct opportunity to turn guests into
regulars, as well as riding the waves of momentum in the
ministry.

One word of warning: Do not drown in the high tide.

Unless you are prepared with correct ratios of volunteers,
facility set up, and resources such as food and drinks, a very
positive time could turn into a struggle and ultimately hurt the

ministry. Again, high tides as well as low tides are causes for us to prepare differently.

When I am explaining this philosophy to youth ministers, I often hear them make the false dichotomy of good times and bad times in their ministry instead of high and low tides. Do not do this! Neither are bad; they are both good! In low tides (not bad times) we have the distinct opportunity to be with our students in different ways. These times provide for more intimate ministry and student leadership opportunities. It is in these times that you can discover some amazing treasures in these relationships and in watching your students lead. A lower attendance period is a great time to let your students cut their teeth at leading Bible studies, doing talks, and participating in other leadership opportunities.

The smaller crowd, which is usually also a more core crowd, provides a place that is less intimidating and more full of grace for them to practice leadership. These are also great times to show your more core group how much you value them. Surprise them with a special night occasionally during these times. It will not only show them how you value them, but it will also be an added bonus for those coming when others, for whatever reasons, are not there. These can be small gestures, such as bringing ice cream, playing an extra game, or switching up programming for that night. This not only creates a sense of importance in the community, but also makes students feel really happy that they came that night.

What about Ministry on a Lake?

I recognize that many of you who are reading this might be thinking that your ministry's ebb and flow looks more like a lake than an ocean. This usually occurs in smaller church youth ministries. Often in these settings high tide looks like about 13 students, and low tide is about eight. While it is a significant shift in regards to percentage, it does not translate in the same way as a larger church going from 100 in high tide to 60 in low tide. So this section is for all you lake dwellers! When you think about your ebb and flow, think about it more from the perspective of understanding what the overall mood and demeanor of the group is in that season.

Just because you do not have major fluctuations in numbers does not mean that you need to keep an unnuanced week in, week out program in place. In some cases your job is even more difficult than that of someone who sees the more major shifts.

In these church settings, the ebb and flow will often come more around the natural seasons of the year. Summer is often a time when it becomes much more difficult to have youth group. With families being gone on different weeks for vacation, your group can be cut in half simply because three families decide to take the same week for summer vacation. This can be not only pretty disheartening, but the morale of the ministry can really take a blow. When you are in a "lake" church, make sure you add these steps when you are planning your ministry calendars each year.

- Find out the families' vacation schedules each summer and over holiday breaks. With a smaller number of families with which to work, it can be much easier just to ask them when they are planning on being gone so that you can plan activities, at least partially, around their dates. The parents in your ministry will not only appreciate this, but it gives you an opportunity to promote the summer happenings with them and make sure that they have your major events on *their* calendars as well.

- Combine with other churches for some fun larger group events. There are several churches in my area that do this incredible ministry together each summer. Each week throughout the summer they gather with five other churches to play different survivor-style games together. They compete as a youth group against other youth groups. However, they design it in such a way that, whether you have five or fifteen youth show up, the ground is even for all groups. It is not only a really phenomenal way to provide your smaller group with a larger group experience but it also builds some great unity among your kids and helps them be proud to represent your church.

- Change the setting. If you are meeting in a room that is built for, and usually has, 15 kids, but you know that attendance is going to run at around five kids each week during the summer, then change your meeting space. You can do this in a couple of ways. One is to actually physically rearrange the space. Make it more intimate so that it feels more full. This can be as simple as moving chairs closer together or moving to a different room, such as a Sunday school room. The other option is to actually move your meeting to a place off of the campus of the church. Coffee shops, ice cream stores, and parks are great places to get your group together for your regular meeting time and provide a fun and different setting that will take their eyes off of who is *not* there and focus on the great time they are having with who *is* there.

- Lastly, change your program. During the summer is a great time to change some of the dynamics of your programs. If you are used to doing a big, up front type of talk during the school year to 15 students, change it to a small group discussion for the five that are there during the summer. Also, if there are programs that your students simply do not attend during the summer, do not be afraid to stop having them and see if an alternative program that is more summer friendly could be added somewhere else. If you choose to do this, make sure to work with your senior pastor and parents in doing so. You do not want to kill a sacred cow in your church unknowingly.

Ministry Is Not the Only Thing That Ebbs and Flows

Finally, remember that your ministry and students are not the only things that ebb and flow. You have to remember that your life, and the lives of parents, volunteers, and adults, involve a constant series of cycles that can produce fatigue or energy, excitement or disappointment, motivation or lethargy. I say this because, in order to do good ministry, we have to be acutely aware of ours and of other systems at work in and around our ministry. When the tide is out in some of the lives of parents in your ministry, you might experience a higher frequency of anxiety and complaints from parents. When this happens—and it will—you have to know how to respond, all the while knowing that this could very well be a difficult time for those around you.

Listen to What They Are Saying and Not Saying

I always try to listen to what people are telling me with their mouths. I want to honor the issue or problem that they are bringing to me, and I want to address it. However, we are human, all of us. Because we are human, it is rare that we are completely self-aware enough to be able to process through and present the many complex layers behind what we are actually feeling and why we feel that way. We should not expect any more from the parents or students with whom we work. So, someone might bring a problem to you and you think to yourself, "Are you kidding me? I have talked about this a million times; they know better!" or, "I work my tail off and this person wants to talk about this one tiny bit of minutia?"

Pause.

Breathe.

Now, look beyond the specifics of what they said and to the deeper fear or anxiety that they are feeling. A comment like, "The youth group doesn't do anything that is fun," can now be deciphered to tell us that this parent's youth is feeling disconnected and the parent wants, desperately, to get the youth back involved, and the parent thinks something "fun" will help with that. Or, "We need to do more programs; we do not offer enough for our kids," can often be translated into: "My kid has an overbooked schedule and it conflicts with the ten programs that you offer weekly; however, I believe if you offer just one more program between 7:42 p.m. and 8:09 p.m. on the third Tuesday of each quarter, my youth will finally be able to come." The bottom line is, they want their kids to be in the youth group, but they have overcommitted and want to fix that. Always look deeper; there is usually something more significant behind the words.

Respond, Do Not React

When you believe you know what is behind the words respond to that thing. Not in an accusatory way or I am smarter than you way (that is a good way to make a ministry long enemy from a concerned parent) but in a caring pastoral way address both their specific concern as well as what you believe is the deeper more root concern. You have to do this with self differentiation while being a non anxious presence. You must also keep you head and not take their remarks or complaints personally, even if they are. If you take them personally you will never be able to rise above the situation and seek a greater solution. Respond to their concerns, DO NOT find yourself in an argument about the minutia.

You Might Be in a Cycle Yourself

Last, remember that you and I are both human too. We get off kilter too. We start pushing buttons that we have no business pushing, which, in our right, non-anxious minds, we would not push. So if you feel convicted that "none of your kids read their Bibles enough," or that "the real reason we are not growing is the minister doesn't go to the water park with the kids each summer and I feel the need to be the prophet who sets them straight," remember to take a step back, breathe, and take a deeper look at your own cycles. So often we are guilty of projecting our internal struggles on those around us, which makes sense. We are human too.

9

Digging Deep without Burying Yourself

I recently wrote an open letter to parents; it has created a considerable amount of buzz and it is a great place to start this conversation.

Dear Parents,

We love your kids.
We love them enough to send you this letter.
Your youth are in a bad place. We have never seen a generation of teenagers who are more stressed, full of anxiety, depressed, suicidal, over-committed, over-medicated, over-worked and over–extra-curriculared, and it is killing them, sometimes literally. We know you want the best for them: the best grades, the best colleges, the best teams, performances, standardized scores, friend groups, etc. We all want the best for them. But they are not the best at everything, and they will never be the best at everything.

I was not, you were not, and they will not stand atop the podium in every area they compete. As I watch the Olympics I have thought a lot about what it takes to get to the Olympics, let alone what it takes to get to the top of that podium. It takes incredible amounts of raw talent, dedication, work, and single-mindedness about that discipline.

Unfortunately, we see many parents pushing these standards and unrealistic expectations in every area of their kids' lives. They cannot do it all; they cannot handle the stress and are being crushed under the weight of the expectation. Now, please hear me; this involves not just your expectations, this involves the expectations of their coaches, teachers, administrators, potential colleges—and the expectations of each other. Expectations are good; they cause us to rise above where we, alone, would usually strive. But they must be realistic expectations based on each student.

Your kids are probably not going to Harvard, and that is okay.

Your kids are probably not going to play a professional sport, and that is okay.

But your kids can be amazing, productive, courageous, and wonderful human beings who love, and have passions and dreams; should we really want more than that?

Our culture is moving to a place where parents are told that they are not allowed to be the ones who determine the limits and expectations of their kids.

When kids come home with 3+ hours of homework every night, you should not accept that; it is not reasonable.

When kids have to practice a sport all summer, every week, so that you cannot take a family vacation or send them on a mission trip because the coach threatens them that they will not play, that is not acceptable.

When you have to beg your kids to get off the computer or video game, or to see their phone, you should remember there should never be any begging involved.

You should set the priorities for your children; you are the ones who determine their schedules; you are the ones who are ultimately responsible for balance in their lives while they are under your roofs. This is not only your right, it is your calling and your responsibility as parents.

You are not powerless in ANY of these situations. Get enough parents together to talk to the administration about the amounts of homework. Pull enough stars from the football team. Disconnect their phones. I guarantee you, that will bring all parties to the table. Now, I am a youth minister. I have been in youth ministry for 16 years. It has not always been this way, trust me. Also, know that when I talk about a balanced life, I am not excluding their spirituality.

There was an article written a few months back that compared youth ministry and church to an elective or extra-curricular. I think that is generous at best.

Most parents and students take electives and extra-curriculars much more seriously than they do regular involvement in a faith community.

Now, do not get me wrong; the lip service is there. "I want to be at youth group on Sunday night, but I have too much homework," "I wish my child could go on the mission trip, but he has football," "I really want them to be in church, but they just have too many things going on right now."

Let's stop playing the game.

If you really want them there, you can make it happen. If a student really wants to be at church or youth group, homework will not get in the way; it doesn't get in the way of basketball, show choir, or ACT prep classes.

Why?

Because we value those things, we love those things, and we are committed to those things.

I will argue you that we are over-investing in each of these things, and are under-investing in the long-term spirituality of our youth. If it is a priority, them make it one; if not, that is okay, but do not make excuses about it. We will respect you a lot more if you do not apologize about your priorities and often try to make us feel bad that your student cannot find one hour a week to come to one of the ten things we offer.

Balance also means not creating kids who spend every waking moment at church. We are not asking you to have them there five times a week. They need other communities, activities, and things that balance their lives. *Sports, academics, the arts, etc., are all wonderful things as long as they are balanced.*

We want you and your student(s) to commit to one or two things a week that will feed them spiritually and give them the opportunity to engage in a community of faith, the way their faith calls them to. Youth group junkies are not what we are trying to create, and is not why this article is written.

Finally, we want to tell you that we know it is hard. We know these decisions are not easy and you have the enormous weight of cultural and societal expectation bearing down on you. But know this...

We as youth ministers and clergy are here to help you. To support you. To join with you as we push back against this culture of excess and strive to bring sanity back to our kids' and our families' lives. We want this—for us, for our communities, and for you. We want families and students and parents to have sabbath, not so you can refuel but so you can rest. We want balance, not so you can add church onto your list of to do's but so you can have time and bandwidth to live out your faith. We want this, not to make you feel guilty, but to help you reclaim your kids' lives, their schedules and your calendars. Ultimately we want this because we love you, we see you suffering, and we want to help.

Let's do this together.

Youth Minister as Prophet (Scary Thought, Right?)

I wrote this letter early one morning in the spring. I had been thinking about it for around a year and, finally, one morning, I could no longer keep it in. It was incredible how quickly it took off. In just a few hours it was averaging over 100 hits a minute, and was making its rounds all over my city. By midday I was getting e-mail from all over the country.

"Thank you, I am a parent who is caught in this system; I thought I was the only one."

"I am told by everyone else (school, athletics, etc.) what fills my calendar; thanks for giving me the permission to take it back."

It was incredible how quickly the response to the post grew. It told me very quickly that the post had hit a nerve with thousands of parents all over the nation.

What I am concerned with is that we are seeing a major problem in family culture in our country, and you, dear reader, are one of the solutions to that problem. Most of this book to this point has dealt with a systemic yet organic way to approach youth ministry. This chapter is a little different. This is a chapter about our prophetic role in youth ministry.

You have a unique position as a youth minister. You are one of the few connection points between multiple generations of the church. If you are doing good youth ministry, you are in contact with the parents in the ministry just as much as you are with the students. You not only have an open line to the students but to the parents as well. This unique position allows you to see families, their successes and challenges, from a pretty important position.

I included the letter I wrote for two reasons. The first is because, from my work as a youth minister and a national consultant, I can see this is a major problem affecting youth and families all over the country. The second is to reemphasize the importance of our being called to be prophetic in our ministries. Remember, prophets in the Old Testament were not simply fortune tellers, they were men and women who were called by God to observe a culture and help that culture see whether it was heading down a destructive path, and just where that path was leading if they did not make some pretty significant changes. Because of your cross-generational role, you have a significant opportunity to speak into the lives of the families in your congregation.

Prophets, Hometowns, and Not Being a Jerk

The first thing I want to make sure that we all understand is that this idea of being prophetic in youth ministry is not an excuse or means to be a jerk. I cannot tell you how many times I have seen ministers—youth minister and church leaders of all sorts—use this idea and title to be abusive, mean, and bearers of guilt in ministry. That is *not* what we are called to do. The second thing I want to make clear is that this idea of being prophetic is also not a church or youth group growth mechanism. Prophets were agents of liberation, not merchants exchanging one oppressive system for another. And, yes, church can be another oppressive system. So, as you enter into thinking about your role differently, make sure that you are being an agent of change and hope.

When Jesus talked about being prophetic, he made it clear that it is very difficult to be a prophet when you are engrained in a system. Jesus says in Mark 6:4 that it is very difficult to be honored or heard in your own hometown. I believe a lot of the reason for this is because, in your own hometown or among your own people, it can be very difficult to have real perspective. To be prophetic in your role as youth minister, as well as to be effective in ministry, requires you to have a level of separation from those who you minister to. If you are caught up in the same systems and structures that your people are, it can be very difficult to speak with much meaning or perspective. So, in review:

- Gain some separation, so as to gain perspective, from the people who you are ministering with.

- Do not be a jerk. Do not use your words and observations to attack.

- Do not exchange one oppressive structure for another.

- When you are speaking into the lives of the people around you, make sure that it is not with the ulterior motive of growing your ministry. God is bigger than their situations, but God is also bigger than your ministry.

Steps to a More Prophetic Ministry

Listen

One of the biggest mistakes youth ministers make is that they come into a youth ministry and community and begin spouting off all of the things that are wrong with that community. I have seen it time and time again. A youth minister will come into a new ministry situation and begin overlaying his or her value system on top of the people in that ministry.

I knew of a church where a new youth minister came in and one of his big values was having lots of praise and worship as a part of the life of the youth ministry. The problem was that the youth ministry did not have the same value. They were very passionate students who loved, God but they were not a group that worshiped God by singing for 30-40 minutes as a part of their worship service. This was not bad; this was not good; it was simply their DNA. This youth minister came in and immediately diagnosed that the youth group "did not know how to worship."

As he entered into the first months of his ministry he continued to focus on this. He lasted less than a year in that ministry, and left angry and without having built any relationships with students or parents. It was not a good situation.

The most important thing a youth minister can do is listen.

Throughout the Old Testament you hear a common refrain from God and the prophets: "I heard the cries of my people." If you listen in your ministry, and listen well, the needs will become evident. It is not only what the people are saying, it is also what they are not saying.

In my situation, I rarely heard the youth talk about being over-programmed, but I also did not hear any sort of joy in what they *were* doing. As I talked with students, they did not like their sports anymore, and were just going through the motions in playing them. I did hear from parents that they were so tired of everyone else's priorities taking control of their families schedules. I heard these things building over the course of a couple of years before I wrote the letter.

Listening is also important because so many times you are one of the only ones all of the parents will speak to. Many times, they will not speak to each other, but will talk to you as their minister. When you hear parents saying the same things over and over, but they do not hear each other saying these things, you have the opportunity/calling to be the one who unifies the voices and helps them know that they are not alone.

Imagine

Sometimes I become frightened that we have lost our prophetic imagination in youth ministry. Again, throughout the Bible, God, Jesus, and the prophets call us to imagine a different way. They constantly call people out of their realities and into a prophetic imagination in which the world that God imagines is translated into realities through the simple actions and words of God's people.

> The task of prophetic ministry is to nurture, nourish and evoke a consciousness and perception alternative to the consciousness and perception of the dominant culture around us. —Walter Brueggemann

I find that in youth ministry we spend too much of our time reacting to what is and forget to imagine what the world could be. Modern prophets like Martin Luther King Jr. call us to dream of a new world in much the same way that the prophets of the Old Testament did. We are, as youth ministers, called into that same prophetic imagining tradition.

Too often, we find ourselves in youth ministry reacting to the circumstances and situations around us. That is not the function of a prophet. When we are using our prophetic imagination, we do not create solutions—we imagine new realities, God's realities. The practical solution to the overscheduling of our kids' lives is to cut back on scheduling, prioritize, and push back against the system. The prophetic imagining comes into play when we reimagine, and help our families reimagine our systems and standards of self-worth.

I am convinced that the reason why our families and students continue to run themselves—and allow themselves to be run—into the ground is because deep inside we do not believe that we are good enough. We believe that we are what we do, and we have not done enough to measure up. What if we reimagined how we understood ourselves and our lives? What if we stopped and realized that we are not what we do, no matter what those around us say?

See, this is not reacting and coming up with solutions to immediate problems; it is a reimagining of the entire system in which we are involved. When I want to tap into that imagination, I always turn to Matthew, chapters 5—7. I cannot think of a better place than the Sermon on the Mount to remain and challenge our current standards and realities. Find that inspiration, and begin living in and giving others the opportunities to live in to those new realities.

Speak and Write

Speak and write. Here is why both are so important. We live in an age of the almighty "Forward" and "Share." These are two powerful tools of revolutions, both good and bad. When we have conversations about these ideas, those conversations mean a lot. Those thoughts and words ripple in the minds of those who participate in those conversations. They can inspire, and can echo from one conversation to the next.

I can tell you, and I am sure you would agree, that there are certain conversations that we have all had throughout our lives that stick with us today and have truly revolutionized who we are and how we think. Speaking in a public way about these prophetic topics is also wildly important. You cannot have an effective civil rights movement without "I Have a Dream" and "The Promised Land" sermons. One of the greatest fuels of mass movements can come from a charismatic speaker who pushes the agenda forward with the art of the spoken word.

At the same time, we cannot forget the power of the written word. Take the Protestant Reformation, for example. I am a firm believer that the Protestant reformation would not have worked a hundred years earlier. Without the newly found place of the printing press in Western European society, Luther and his followers would have never had the means by which to get out their message. It is amazing that we now live in a world where each one of us has access to the modern printing press we call the Internet. From social-media–funded revolutions in the Middle East, to organic grassroots blog-funded movements here, the Internet has given everyone a platform and voice.

Never in the history of humanity has this sort of mass communication medium been available and available to all. It is incredible (and a little scary) that you and I have the exact same access to spreading our messages out into our world as political leaders, world figures, and celebrities. The Internet is, as of now, an equal-access platform.

I sat in my study early one morning in February, typed out the letter to parents, and, within an hour, one thousand people had already read it. In no other time in history was that possible. Because it was a written communication, it was able to be passed around, forwarded, copied and pasted, printed, and even snail mailed all over the country and the world. Speaking alone does not do that. There is something about having a tangible word that people can not only grab on to but pass along as well.

Support

Last, we cannot lead these sorts of changes in the lives of our families and churches unless we are committed to the pastoral as much as we are committed to the prophetic. Too often, youth ministers love being the fiery preachers who drop "the word of the Lord" on people and ride off into the sunset, leaving someone else to clean up the mess. This is not only ineffective, it is also irresponsible. People do not change at the drop of a hat. Even when people are excited about the ideas we propose, they still have to be nurtured and walked alongside in these small revolutions. Revolutions that last can only come through relationships.

Now, relationships are not merely utilitarian. That would encourage an abuse of trust and position. Relationships are where people's hearts are changed and can grow. It is through trust and mutuality that people find the safety to think outside of their current paradigms and find the courage dip their toes into a new world. Relationships are not only the places where revolutions come to fruition, they are also where revolutions start.

You have to be in good, deep, trusting relationships with your youth and the parents from the beginning, long before you ever speak hard but liberating words. If you are only interested in stepping into situations, laying down your "truths," and walking away, please do not stay in youth ministry. That is not what families need and, to be honest, not what the church needs. Families and churches need people who are it this for the journey, not the moment.

Brian McLaren in *A New Kind of Christian* talks about major changes in history and societies are always fueled by a new technology that changes how we communicate. There has never been a time like now to reclaim our prophetic imaginations. Remember too that each of us only have a certain amount of capital from which to speak. We cannot go around each week with a new "cause." We have to be good stewards of this trust and make sure, through prayer and open ears and minds, to act when we are called, not only when we become passionate about something. Also, remember that every change that you see needs to happen has to happen right now or has to happen because of you. We are all in this together; trust God, and trust each other that we each have our parts to play.

10

Organic Relationships

In 2007 Andy Root released his first and arguably most influential book, *Revisiting Relational Youth Ministry*. In this book he takes our traditional understandings of youth ministry and our presumptions of their relational nature and turns them on their head. It was and is a book that continues to inspire and challenge how I do youth ministry today. One of his primary points is that we have to move away from the "influencer" model and practice of youth ministry and into a "space sharing" methodology. In this he argues that the best youth ministry is not when we are in relationships whose goal is to change and influence students' behavior and habits. While this has been our traditional model, Root has no qualms about claiming that it is not only ineffective but also detrimental to our students.

While this understanding is critical to ministry with youth, we also have to understand that it is also critical to how we enter into relationships with parents and volunteers. For far too long youth ministry has viewed parents, volunteers, and to some extent the entire church as secondary and tertiary components to the ministry we do with students. Because of the work of scholars such as Kenda Creasy Dean, Christian Smith, Kara Powell, and others, we know two very important facts that were not available ten years ago:

- Over 70 percent of a student's spiritual influence comes directly from the parents. (National Study of Youth and Religion)

- The more adult relationships we can provide and facilitate for our students, the more likely they will become more deeply ingrained in the life of the church, also resulting in a higher rate of church involvement in their own adulthood.

Youth ministries who do not know, adopt, and work within this understanding will not only struggle with long-term discipleship, but they will also continue to foster a faith in students that is juvenile in its understanding and practice, as well as lacking any roots in the greater ecclesial body.

There is one sad truth as to why this happens in youth ministries: most youth ministers are uncomfortable with (if not downright scared of) other adults.

What I continue to find are youth ministers, young and old, who simply do not know how to talk with, be in relationship with, or work with adults. This makes sense if you think about it. Most youth ministers got into the profession because they love working with youth, not adults. The thought has been, "If you want to work with adults, be a pastor, if you want to work with youth, be a youth pastor."

Common sense, right?

Wrong.

If you got into youth ministry to only work with youth, I want you to do one of two things:

- Get another, better-paying job and volunteer with your local youth ministry. You will make more money, and will be much more successful as a volunteer in ministry. Or…

- Start understanding your job as being just as much about adult and parent ministry as it is youth ministry.

If you choose the latter, which I hope you do, there are some steps that will aid you in this ministerial transition.

- You are a professional; act like one. Long gone are the days of sloppy communication, immature relationships, "forgetfulness," unorganized calendars, and planning on the fly. Parents no longer have the time or bandwidth to put up with this type of ministry, and no longer should they.

- They are not out to get you; at least, most of them are not. Granted, you might cross a parent the wrong way sometimes and a grudge might develop. But the majority of a youth minister's problems come from not being proficient and disciplined in the ministry. If you can get that under control, you will dramatically decrease the number of complaints you have. There will still be complaints, and there is a way you have to handle those, which leads me to the final point.

- You are an adult, not a youth. This is often one of the most difficult things for youth ministers to understand. It is often something that parents will defend in their youth ministers: "We want someone who can relate to the kids, someone who is on their level." Let's address that statement: You can be an adult and be able to relate to your students. Youth ministry depends on that fact. Not only does youth ministry depend on it, but so do our schools, sports teams, the arts, parenting, and any other mechanism in which youth are involved. We have to quit acting like church is the one place where we want to encourage leadership that is not conducive to nurture, growth, and the forward movement of the students into their next reality: adulthood. Be different.

If you are being a professional and working with parents and adults on *their* levels, reducing the "us versus them" mentality and being an adult yourself, you will find yourself well on your way to doing wonderful relational (adult) ministry.

The Commoditization of Relationships

Commodity—a good for which there is demand, but which is supplied without qualitative differentiation across the market. While this language is not often used when talking about students, parents, and volunteers, it's methodology and practice is often prevalent in how we think and treat people in our ministry. I have both seen and practiced this unfortunate methodology in regards to parents and adults in ministry. So often, when a youth minister gets past the fear of working with parents, the minister ends up seeing them as a means to an end, a ratio quota, or another "warm body."

I can promise you that your ministry will live and die on the volunteers you put into place. Trust me, I have experienced the best and the worst of this reality. You are much more likely to experience the worst of this paradigm if you are not personally invested in the volunteers, their ministry, and their lives. Jason Gant, the former youth minister at the largest United Methodist Church in the country, would often talk about this investment being the most important thing we can do as youth ministers. But, remember, this is not an investment so that we can have them do our bidding; that is utilitarian. This is an investment in the same way I bring my wife flowers, hug her when she is sad and ask her how her day was. It is an investment in a relationship that matters intrinsically, not because of a secondary purpose.

Unfortunately, many relationships that I see in student ministries are based on a philosophy that is purely utilitarian in nature. The parents need the youth minister to do the work they do not want, or feel ill-equipped, to do; the youth minister needs the parents because either the minister cannot handle all of the students, he or she need drivers, or the pastor or a pesky consulting organization, www.ministryarchitects.com, is saying a certain number of adults is required in ratio to the number of students. When this dichotomy is the basis for partnerships in youth ministry, problems are bound to arise.

Finally, one of the most common problems the commoditization of relationships continues to cause is a general distrust as to whether the youth minister is pulling their weight in the ministry. This distrust can lead to a tug and pull for resources, time, and priority. I have also seen it result in parents taking an overbearing role in youth ministries, deciding to "take the bull by the horns" because of what they are perceiving as an underperforming youth minister, which creates splinters in the ministry of the church to the youth. Despite how both parties feel, no one suffers more than the very youth each group is fighting to serve. The two-way commoditization of relationships makes ministering to youth not only very difficult, but also a burden on all who participate.

This dualistic ministry and encampment approach is not the only, and is certainly not the best, way to approach ministry with youth in the church. The better way not only involves work and commitment from both the staff and the adult volunteers, it also necessitates humility, diversity, and a willingness to embrace that we are better together.

The Priesthood of Adulthood

One of the most important and controversial doctrines to come from the Protestant Reformation is the idea that each individual can and should approach the text personally—reading, interpreting, and applying it as the Holy Spirit leads. No longer was ministry centered in the clergy. The priesthood of all believers not paved the way to a plethora of new and important voices in interpretation of the Scriptures, it also gave impetus to the laity to go, do, and serve. The work and ministry was now in the hands of the people, and Christianity changed forever.

Unfortunately, youth ministry has been slow to adopt these practices fully. In most youth ministries parents are invited to help the youth minister. Many times this plays out, at best, as the adult being a warm-bodied gopher. When we do not recognize and enable the unique and God-given gifts of those adults who are around us, then we have no right being in ministry with youth.

One of our primary jobs must be the job of recognizing, empowering, and enabling adults to do the ministry of the church. If you are a mainline church, this approach is not only good youth ministry, but you are empowering these adults to live into the covenant that they made at the baptism of their child. When you are not doing this, you are hindering one of their callings as people of faith in a covenantal relationship with God. I know that is heavy, but it is a reality of the importance of the ministry that we are called to.

I also know that doing this can be very hard work. In many churches, I work with adults who do not want to work with the youth. This is especially prominent in small churches. If a small church can afford a youth minister, they often will completely outsource the youth ministry to that person. When you have a youth group of 10–15 people, the need for more adults to meet certain ratio is not as necessary. It can often be much more difficult to recruit adults because there are far fewer to choose from, especially if the church's average congregant's age is higher.

Small churches have a distinct opportunity, however, to embody the youth ministry in the whole life of the congregation. In the best-case scenarios, the whole church understands itself as youth volunteers and mentors. The lines between youth group and church are very blurred, and it makes for amazing ministry. So while this can be a unique problem for smaller churches, if reimagined, it can turn into a unique asset!

2 Ways to (Re)Ordain Adults for Ministry

- *Help them hear their calling*—First and foremost, the adults of your church have to understand and, more importantly, *feel* a calling to the youth ministry. One of the best ways to do this is to introduce them to students. I cannot tell you how many adults I have been able to bring into larger, sustained roles in my youth ministry because I gave them a simple, noncommittal way to spend some time with our students. I have had so many people come up to me after and say, "Those kids were great! That was a lot of fun." Then I proceed to tell them how I saw them thrive with the students, and invite them into another opportunity. After spending some time with the youth, they begin to feel drawn and, ultimately, called to work with the youth of their church.

- *Help them remember*—One of the principles of the Jewish calendar, with its feasts and festivals, is to call its people continually to remember. They are called to remember their bondage in Egypt, how YHWH called them and delivered them out of Egypt and into a promised land. Remembering is an important sustaining part of the Jewish faith, as well as in Christianity. When God called the Israelites, God not only called them out of bondage but also called them into covenant. We as people of faith, especially in mainline traditions, are called into covenant each time we baptize a child. In each mainline tradition, the baptismal covenant is committed to by the congregation—that they will be partners in raising the child in the ways and life of Christ. As youth ministers we have to constantly help people remember, just as the prophets would help the Israelites remember, their covenantal promises to and for these children. I also find it particularly helpful to remind adults of their time as youth. When adults grew up in a youth group you have an entire well of emotional and sentimental memories from which to draw. Help them remember those incredible trips, the retreats, youth group meetings, and especially help them remember the volunteers and adults who poured their time and energy into them as youth. Help them remember those special relationships and how they are called to be the adults in those stories now. Their covenant calls them into those nurturing and challenging relationships with youth and calls them to mentor the students of their church. Help them remember, and help them look forward to who and what they can be to the students whose faith they have been entrusted with.

When we understand and help other adults understand that it is their covenantal role and calling to be part of youth ministry, we can begin to develop some pretty significant partnerships with them in ministry. We have to be very clear that we are co-ministers with our adults in this ministry, and make sure that they do not see a dichotomy in the roles. When we move to this sort of model, we also move from subservient warm bodies and utilitarian relationships, and into real and shared incarnational ministry. This sort of ministry is also a ministry among friends and colleagues.

The Importance of Peculiarity in Ministry

One of the bases of this ministry style also involves "doing life" with your volunteers. In order to be fully faithful in our calling as ministers, we also have to remember that our ministry relationships extend beyond our students and to our volunteers. In this way we also have to be fully invested in the lives, passions, hurts, joys, and failures of our volunteers. These can be incredible partnerships and friendships in the often lonely world of ministry. I have done life, death, marriage, and divorce with my volunteers. I have been with them as they welcomed babies into the world and as they later sent those children off to college. I have also seen youth graduate, go off to college, and come back to be volunteers in the ministry they love. For a youth minister, and especially a youth minister with some longevity, these relationships can be some of the greatest and most unexpected gifts in the ministry we do with youth.

I will offer one word of warning.

Even as we invest in those relationships with our volunteers, we have to remember that we are still called to a peculiar role in ministry. We are still called to be people who, even in and beyond those relationships, can speak to our people in ways that call them beyond where they are and into the new realities of where God is calling them. This can be difficult the longer we are in ministry in one place. It is so easy for us to become more and more homogenous with our people the more we know and love them.

As I write this I am on a plane flying from Austin, Texas, to my home in Birmingham. If you have ever been to Austin you will know that one of the things that makes it unique is its catchy and wildly popular motto, "Keep Austin Weird." I cannot help but think that this is a motto we in youth ministry must adopt and recite on a regular basis to ourselves. In order to continue to be effective and helpful to the people we serve, we have to stay peculiar or weird. I do not mean to do this is a way that is obnoxious or holier than thou. I mean it in the way the Old Testament prophets were just a little different, just a little weird. They never fit in all the way with their contemporaries, always being slightly different and, in time, effective.

Keep youth ministers weird.

Passions First, Positions Second

Now down to the nuts and bolts.

Intentional friendships, co-ministering, and incredible partnerships. Yes, yes, and yes. The important part to remember is that none of this can happen unless we first get these people in the right positions and serving with our students. There are a number of incredible recruiting methods, systems, and processes. Use them. I especially recommend Mark DeVries and Nate Stratman's book *The 30-Day Change Project*. While I am very much a systems person and love to build ministry structures in and around volunteer recruiting, that is not what this section is about. This is about the heart of the recruiting process. I cannot express to you how important it is to get adults into positions that they can be passionate about. When an adult is in a position that he or she is passionate about, you will not only see your volunteer's longevity shoot through the roof, you will also help him or her know what it feels like to be in that sweet spot where you are doing the ministry that God has equipped you to do. In order to be able to do this, you have to first do a few other things.

- *Know Your Adults*—This might seem silly; "Well, of course I know my adults." I am not talking about knowing their names and what families they belong to, but *really* knowing them: their history, gifts, and fears.

- *Talk with Your Adults*—Again, rudimentary on the surface, but significant in the details. You have to talk with your volunteers outside of those small conversations on Sunday mornings. Talk with them about their experiences and where they have experienced God most in the church and outside of the church.

- *Dream for and with Your Adults*—Dream about where you could see them thrive. Dream about where you could see them doing ministry and even ministry better than you could do it. Dream about where their passions meet your student's needs. Dream inside your current program and dream into the future of your program. Then dream about all of these things with your adults. Help them see themselves doing what God has made them to do, and help them see themselves doing in your program.

So many times I hear youth ministers talk about feeling guilty when they are in their volunteer recruitment season. So often they end up recruiting with this same type of enthusiasm. Stop feeling guilty. If you are engaging in real relationships with your volunteers—enabling, not using, and helping them find their calling in youth ministry—you are giving them a gift. Think about it like this. Do you remember when you first realized that God was calling you into ministry? Do remember those people who helped you, encouraged you, and showed you how to be the best minister you could be?

Remember?

Now go and do that for those co-ministers who will join with you in doing incredible youth ministry.

11

Eliminating Preservatives

Growing up in the country had some disadvantages: few restaurants, having to drive a long way into town, packs of wild dogs, and swarms of mosquitoes. The last two were not usually encountered together, but both were pretty scary.

It also had some pretty great advantages, such as beautiful star-filled skies that only exist outside city lights, calm afternoons when the only noise is a cool southern breeze rustling the leaves, and fresh homegrown fruits and vegetables.

Now, I know living in the country does not automatically mean you have fresh fruits and vegetables at your disposal, but we did. We had a huge garden with rows and rows of corn, tomatoes, potatoes, pumpkins, watermelons, beans, squash, strawberries, cucumbers, onions, blackberries, and loads of other yummy treats. We also had a small grove of fruit trees—apples, mainly. I don't know if you have ever had an apple fresh off the tree before, but it is something special.

We grew a variety of apples, but my favorite were our golden delicious. I remember picking them in the afternoons, usually as a snack before supper. They would hang lazily on the trees, just waiting to be plucked from their branches and devoured by one hungry barefoot boy. The apples were small and uneven, with dull, pale yellow skin and blemishes abounding. They were not very attractive at all, but it was what I knew, and I knew they tasted amazing!

One of my first memories of grocery shopping was later that year. The store was nothing to brag about but it had what we needed. I remember being in the small produce section of our hometown grocery store walking down the aisle looking at all of the fruits and vegetables. I distinctively remember being amazed at the apple section. They were huge! Beautiful red, yellow, pink, and green apples, shiny and perfectly shaped, piled high, separated by kind.

I remember picking out one that seemed as big as my head, a giant deep red apple whose skin was spotless and whose shape rivaled any pictures of apples hanging from the walls of my elementary school.

It was perfect.

We checked out, went home, and I remember reaching down into the bag—rummaging around desperately, seeking by juicy treasure.

I found it; I did not wait; I dove in like it was a pool on the first day of summer. I took a big bite...then...

My brow crinkled, my chewing slowed, and total disappointment washed over my face. My beautiful, perfect apple was grainy, waxy, and had very little of the deep, rich, sweet taste that I had come to expect from the apples that I picked in my front yard.

Was I sad? Yes, a little.

Was I mad? Not really.

To be honest, more than anything, I was confused.

How could something so beautifully perfect have so little substance?

The Problem with Growing Perfect Fruit

I knew this pastor once. He was good. His suits were crisp, his hair tight, and his words were always perfectly placed and timed. He was good. I remember thinking to myself: *This guy*

is someone that I should really pay attention to. He had a way
with people. He seemed to know exactly what to say, when to
say it, and how to say it. He even had this smile: it made you
feel confident of nothing else other than that you wanted to
continue to hang out with this guy because he had it together.
His life was good. He was good.

To be honest I have known a lot of people in ministry who
fit that description. They exude this almost perfect, sort of holy,
"aura." People cannot help but lift them up as an example of
what it means to a Christian.

I used to idolize these people. I saw them as some sort of
archetypal goal of what a minister should be, what I wanted
to be. The interesting thing is that these people always let me
down, and, often, let me down hard. Fraud, affairs, unethical
practices, the list could go on and on. Each time I thought I
had found someone to believe in, to follow, I would soon learn
about just how imperfect that person was.

As I became older I realized that my disappointment did not
stem so much from their actions as from the disparity between
what and who I believed them to be, and who they actually
turned out to be. They fell so far because they had been placed—
or, more often than not, they had placed themselves—so high
above everyone else. This was a cycle that I had seen with so many
of my heroes and that, truthfully, I feared it would overtake me
as well. I was so scared because it was the only model I knew.

As someone working toward being a minister (by the
way, if you are reading this book because you want to work
or are working with youth, you *are* a minister), I thought this
perfection model was what we were expected to do and was the
most effective way to be in ministry. It was even explained to
me by one of these ministers: "You have to live life like you are
in a glass house and be perfect; you are the example that they
should try to live their lives towards. If you struggle or show
weaknesses, they will think that their weaknesses are okay too."

So I tried to be perfect.

I beat myself up when I was not, and I beat others up
(metaphorically) when they were not as well.

This was not just a perfection in regards to how I lived my
life, it was also a theological perfection—I had to have a solid

answer for *everything*. Again, if I did not, then what sort of minister was I? I used verses such as, "Study to show yourself approved," like a flogging device for self-flagellation. I could never know enough and could never do enough, and if I held others to that standard as well, I might be able to keep the game going.

I am guessing you are not in a situation quite an neurotic as I was, but I would bet at least some of what I just wrote resonates loud and clear with you in your ministry. Pressure, anxiety, guilt, never amounting to anything, never clocking out, never being able to make a mistake... Sound familiar?

The Beautiful Blemishes, or Learning to Be Human

For me, this sort of ministry approach came to a head around my sophomore year of college. I was starting to realize that nothing about this type of approach to ministry was sustainable. The problem was that it was still the only real approach to ministry that I knew and since it was my only paradigm, it was making me really rethink whether ministry was even an option any longer.

Then it happened.

I was in a preaching class taught by my now friend, then professor, Dr. Barnette. Dr. Barnette is an incredible professor because he is an incredible guy. Dr. Barnette had grown up around great preachers, and one of his favorites was an Episcopal priest, Dr. John Claypool. John was originally a Southern Baptist minister until the untimely death of his little girl, Laura Lue, who happened to be a friend of Dr. Barnette when he was a little boy. When she was diagnosed with leukemia, John had to make a decision. He could either stand in his pulpit on Sunday morning and pretend that the world was good and his belief was solid, or he could be honest, transparent, and live his struggle in the context of his sermons. He chose the latter. Over the course of her disease and ultimately her death, John preached honestly and pastorally. He dealt with his own doubt, his anger with God, and his pain.

He was not strong; he was weak.

He was not polished; he was weathered.

He was not perfect; he was perfectly human.

Several of the sermons during this time were published in a small book called *Tracks of a Fellow Struggler*. My sophomore year of college I was introduced to this beautifully honest and incredibly hopeful book by Dr. Barnette. It was incredibly hopeful not only because of the words of Dr. Claypool but because, for the first time in ministry, I felt like I had a new example of how to do ministry that did not require me to be perfect, or at least work so hard to make people believe so.

For the first time I had someone who, at least through the pages of a book, I could look up to and follow the example of. A few years later I chose my seminary and had the incredible privilege of studying under Dr. Claypool. During that time I learned the full value of what is known as "confessional preaching." It is simply a style of preaching and ministry in which the minister lives in the tension and the struggle of the text and life with the church. John had already had a very tough struggle with cancer himself when we learned that he was suffering from it again.

I was taking "Preaching and the Life of Dr. Martin Luther King" with Dr. Claypool during the most intense of his chemo treatments. His treatments were on Tuesdays and Thursdays, just an hour before we had class each day. He would come in tired, hurting, and sick from his treatments. Each day he would come in and talk with us young seminary students about what it was like to die. He would talk to us about the irony of poisoning your body to heal your body. He talked about chemo as a sacrament, and death as life. Even now I tear up thinking about the beauty of these moments, these last moments we spent with him. He died just a few months later.

He gave us a gift. He allowed us into his struggle. He invited us into a tender place, shared it with us, and allowed us to live in that place and do life in it with him. It was a gift of vulnerability, grace, and hope.

It was perfect.

It was perfect because he knew he did not have to be.

Perfect Student Ministry

Dr. Claypool would always tell us: "Perfection is the highest form of self-abuse." I think the inverse is also true. I think that when we allow ourselves to be imperfect, to struggle, to live in tension, and to do that in community, it can be the highest form of self-care. When done well, it can be one of the most healing forms of student ministry we can do.

The student ministry you run should not be based around you and everything that bothers you, worries you, or makes you lose sleep. That is not what confessional ministry is about. It is also not about processing all of our doubts and questions publicly. It is, however, an unscripted balance of living in the tension of life and Scripture with your students. The tension is not only about your life but about the lives of your students as well.

Perfect student ministry is recognizing and affirming the imperfections in our lives. It is not glossing over and sweeping under the rug the messiness. It is being vulnerable so that your students know that your ministry is a place for vulnerability, confession, and imperfection. It is holding up the mantle that we are, as Nadia Bolz Weber puts it, a church for all saints and sinners. It is helping our students understand that the perfection that Jesus calls us to has little to do with not messing up and everything to do with being perfectly human.

Perfect student ministry occurs when everyone's imperfection is evident, and it is in that space that we find one another and we find our great healer.

Healthy Confessional Student Ministry

We would be naive not to explore some basic guidelines for doing confessional ministry with students in a healthy way. I have seen it done in a very unhealthy way, in which the adult in charge uses youth group or Sunday school as a personal therapy session. If you or someone in your ministry is doing that, stop immediately and find a counselor you can work with personally. If you are confessing in youth group, it is probably because you do not have another outlet, and it is important for your health and the health of your students for you to process with another adult. The line is a little finer when doing this in student ministry. Because their brains are still forming and because they are not adults, it is important we use certain gauges as we work with students. Some are commonsense, while others are a little more nuanced.

- *Off-Limits Topics*—While confessional ministry can be incredibly meaningful and effective, there are some topics that I would recommend generally staying clear of. While I think it is healthy to talk about one's sexual past with students, it has to be done very carefully—and I would recommend doing so with little detail and in general terms. Also, if you are discussing situations of abuse, always remember to do so knowing that there is a very good chance that one or more of the students in your group have encountered abuse. You will want to always make sure that you offer follow-up care with your students so that anyone your discussions might affect will have access to you or another adult.

- *Not Undermining Parents*—I am a firm believer that we, as youth ministers, need to constantly challenge our students. Sometimes when challenging our students, we will inadvertently also challenge things their parents have taught them. This is going to happen sometimes, and it is a natural part of student ministry. The problem comes when we undermine parents intentionally. We have to remember that some of our most important allies in youth ministry are our parents. We are always better together than apart. For this reason, it is crucial that we are communicating with our parents constantly, and *always* keeping them in the loop with everything we are teaching. We do this a number of ways in my student ministry. Each week in the parent newsletter I talk about what we are learning and experiencing. We also always videorecord our talks and put them on our Vimeo site. In the weekly newsletter I include a link to these so the parents and students always have direct access to what we teach. I also use our youth leadership team as a resource to talk through series and topics. Again, remember, your parents are your greatest resource and you have the opportunity to be theirs as well.

- *Too Current*—There are some topics that can be really powerful to talk about while they are happening. As with Dr. Claypool, it can be very impactful to talk about death when it is experienced in your community. When you do so, your pain and the processing of it can be very helpful for others as well. The question you have to ask yourself is, "Can I do it in a way that is helpful and not harmful?" Emotion is good and real; however, if you cannot speak properly because you are overwhelmed with grief, it might be best to allow others to lead. There are also other topics that can be too current to deal with in a productive way. One of the most important things about confessional ministry is being in a place where you can speak about a situation with some perspective. Dr. Claypool was able to do this even in the middle of the dying of his daughter. Most of us are not self-aware enough to be able to do this, so be cautious.

- *Does It Have Theological Value?*—Just because it is important to you or is deeply impacting your life does not mean that it has theological value for your students. Again, sometimes youth ministers are guilty of treating youth group as if it is *their* youth group—full of their peers, to be their community. This is not helpful to you or your students. We only spend a few hours a week at most with our students, so we are not being good stewards of their time if we are inadvertently using it for ourselves. Before employing confessional youth ministry always ask, "What will this do to benefit/ challenge/encourage or teach the students?" If you cannot answer this question quickly and succinctly, it is probably a good idea to hold off on being confessional in that moment.

So many times those of us in ministry are more worried with self-preservation and image keeping. Some of the most important ministry that we can do is ministry that comes from places of pain and honesty. Carl Jung coined the term "Wounded Healer," which was later made more popular in ministry circles by Henri Nouwen. The idea is that we heal because and out of our own hurt and affliction. Some of the most powerful ministry that you can do with your students comes from these places of pain. When utilized appropriately, this ministry can open up conversations and relationships that simple Bible studies and sermons would never come close to. Through time, this practice of ministry can also begin a deeper form of healing—a healing that we never expected—in our own lives as well.

12

Self-Care for Ministers

As I began to lay out this book, I found myself torn on the placement of this chapter. The problem is this chapter is the most important in this entire book and its placement, in my opinion, says a lot about our approach to student ministry. I finally chose to place it at the end of the book as a capstone, not as a foundation. Our student ministries should not be built around us, our talents, or our passions. The student ministries that we are responsible for should always be based on the mission, passion, and calling of the congregation that we serve and serve with. However, in order for us to lead these ministries effectively and to do so in a way that produces joy, fulfillment, and longevity in our own careers, we have to do so in a way that is both healthy and sustainable for us as well. In this final chapter the focus is you: your health, well-being, and spirituality. This is not a chapter about doing this so that your ministry will be healthier or more productive. If it were, that would mean that your life doesn't matter except as a utilitarian piece of the formula for a good student ministry.

That is not about the case.

This chapter is about taking care of yourself—but not for your ministry, not for productivity, not so that you can go harder and do more. It is about taking care of yourself because you are a child of God, and God says you matter. Do not skip this chapter; do not take it as a suggestion. Know and embody this. Take this very seriously. I promise you, some of the most spiritually, physically, and emotionally unhealthy people I encounter are people in ministry. This could be avoided.

I have never known anyone who has gone into ministry with the expressed purpose of burning themselves out, yet it happens all of the time.

Two Great Ways to Burn out in Ministry

There are two primary reasons why I find burnout occurring in student ministers. The first is love: love for our students, for our churches, for parents, and for the practice of student ministry. You have to love this job and those involved in order to get into it. I personally do not know anyone who got into this line of work for the salary, benefits, great hours, or exotic locales. Most people I know got into it because of love: love of students, God, the church, or even their own youth ministry experience.

This love, unless handled with a discerning spirit and a disciplined practice, can kill you. It is so easy to give all of yourself to the practice if student ministry. It is so simple to find yourself putting in way more hours, days, and weekends than you should, all for the sake of love. So often I see youth ministers giving more than they have to give and, consequently, finding themselves completely spent. We all are guilty of this at some point and, for most, at many points in our ministry careers. It is this love of what we do that can, and has for so many in ministry, end careers. Unlike working for a company or a business, most of us feel a deeper sense of connection to the work that we do, and that connection can make it tough to set boundaries and can even produce deep guilt if boundaries are set and held.

Beyond our own love of our profession, the second-biggest reason for burnout is the often unregulated over-consumption of our time and energies by the very people and institutions that we serve. There is one rule to always remember in ministry. The church will rarely tell you to work less, not answer the call or the text when you are at dinner with your family, or keep your Sabbath holy. It is not that the church is evil or that the church wants you to burn out. It really is an issue of self-regulation. When a parent calls you on a Friday night asking for some information that is clearly on your website, she is not doing anything wrong. It's inconvenient. However, that one frustrating phone call, in addition to the two texts at dinner plus the fact that you did not eat dinner with your family Tuesday because of the meeting and Wednesday because of small groups, is cause for a blow-up if you depend on someone else to tell you when enough is enough.

If you learn nothing else from this book, learn this: you are the only one who can say when it is enough. While it does not mean to be, the church can and is in most cases the number one cause for burnout among its ministers. You have to be confident enough in who you are and in your ministry to set these limits and keep them.

The End of "Slash and Burn" Student Ministry

"Slash and burn farming" is the practice of over-farming a piece of land, exploiting it over and over again, to produce the highest yield without regard to its condition or sustainability.

Slash and burn is one of the major models of student ministry that is happening all over the country. In modern youth ministry the lives, health, emotional well being, marriages, spiritual longevity, and vocational callings of youth ministers are constantly being used and abused as expendable resources by both the churches and the youth ministers as fuel to keep the insatiable fire of youth ministry going. The results of this kind of youth ministry are lifeless, cynical shells of burned-out youth ministers strewn about the ministerial landscape of America.

If we are going to move away from this sort of unhealthy ministry, then we who are in youth ministry have to be the ones who initiate it; it has to begin with us.

Below are ways to have a ministry with longevity, life, and fruitfulness—one that will feed you and your church long after the honeymoon is over.

Five Practices for Longevity and Life

1. Remember, Your Job Does Not Define You

One of the best and worst things we as youth ministers can do is to let our jobs define us. When we are successful, have triumphs, and see a ministry grow, doing this can not only be a great confidence booster but can also be an emotional wave that we can ride for a nice little stretch. However, the inverse is also true. When things are not going well, or when parents would rather eat you for Sunday lunch than their fried chicken, these are some of the worst times to let our jobs define us. I can remember these times most vividly because of the heartburn, ulcers, sleepless nights, and the underpinning anxiety that eats away at an otherwise productive ministry.

When all of the chips are on the table, it is very difficult to not let our jobs define us, but it is a temptation that we must constantly fight. One of the best ways I have found to do this is to focus on the other hats I wear. For me, the hats of "father" and "husband" are key in doing this.

I can remember an especially difficult six-month stretch of ministry when my spirit was constantly crushed as work. It was all I could do to drag myself home, but, without fail, I did, and my little girl who was two at the time would run to the door screaming my name as if I had just saved the world from alien invaders. It was, and still is, magical.

That should not be the only thing we hang our hats on, but it is more of a definer of our selves than what we do from 9–5 each day. Find those things that are your definition points, make them your focus, and judge your success not only on your ministerial endeavors but, more importantly, on the things that really matter most in life. Point number 3 below will also help with this.

2. Hone and Sharpen Your Blade

I love cooking and I love watching cooking shows. The other night I was watching a show and the entire episode was dedicated to the importance of sharpening and keeping sharp your knives. Youth ministry functions in much the same way. We know that there is a need, a real need, to hone and sharpen our skills frequently. The difference is that very few of us recognize how important the consistency and frequency are as well.

I am an avid proponent of the idea that we should be reading and taking in as much as we can every day. Some would say that this produces an overload of ideas. If we try to implement everything we learn, then, yes, we would be consumed under an avalanche of material. If, however, we practice reading, grasping, conceptualizing, and a file system, we will thrive in massive amounts of information.

First is reading. I read books on youth ministry, church growth, mission, sociology, theology, philosophy, and business. I always have 2–3 of these books with me to work through. I also subscribe to loads of blogs. These provide me two different sources of material: the established and the innovating. "Grasping" is simply working to understand the ideas and principles the article or chapter is putting forth in such a way that we can sum up what the author is saying in one or two sentences. "Conceptualizing" is when we take those ideas and think how they could possibly work in our own ministry. To make sure we don't simply transplant these ideas, we need to take into consideration context, time, size, and the other factors that make our church unique.

Finally, one of the most important pieces is filing it away! It is very rare that I will take an idea and implement it right into the ministry. It needs time, like a good steak, to rest, letting all of the juices come together and settle. You will be surprised, as I have been, how quickly a "great" idea will turn bad and raise red flags if it is able to just sit for a little while. Hopefully, we are all planning ahead enough that it is difficult for us just drop something in at the last minute anyway.

The second way I like to get away is to go away on continuing education. There are numerous opportunities for continuing education now that youth ministry is such a lucrative business. I have found that, for my money, Princeton Theological Seminary's Institute for Youth Ministry is the best. Being that it is in Princeton, you are automatically provided with a wonderful venue. They bring in the best speakers, theologians, practitioners, and writers in and around the field of youth ministry.

This is a great place to get new ideas, network, learn, and interact with some of the finest minds in the field. It is a highlight of my year in youth ministry. If we are working hard to keep our knowledge and skills sharp, our work will be much more innovative and we are less likely to become bored with what we are doing in ministry.

3. Get a Life!

On the other hand, you also have to have a life. A life outside of youth ministry. I cannot stand to look at a youth minister profile of Facebook and see things such as: Interests—Hanging out with my youth group, reading youth ministry books, four square, and church van rides.

This sort of behavior is unhealthy! We need lives outside of the church campus. We need to eat and enjoy food beyond pizza. We need to read other books than the masterful works of Kenda Dean, Andrew Root, and Doug Fields! We need to get a life.

I know this is a rant, but I think it needs to be. One of the saddest things I see happen to ministers is ministerial identity loss. It is what happens when we totally immerse ourselves in all things "youth ministry" and forget that we actually had lives, loves, passions, interests, and endeavors before we jumped into the great work called youth ministry.

Rekindle these loves and passions, and let them be a wildfire that reignites your love for ministry. Diversify your life portfolio and the dividends will be hearty. Let me tell you what I am passionate about: cooking, reading, writing, photography, traveling and world affairs. If someone walked up to you right now and told you to name what you were passionate about, could you? Could you not only name them without thinking, but cite current specific examples of when you indulged in each? If not, then maybe it is time to get a life!

4. Shape Up!

Health, not the health of the group or spiritual health, but *health*, is one of the most overlooked pieces in the youth minister's life. When your diet is consistently getting major jolts of coffee, pizza, and camp food, it is difficult to figure out ways of maintaining a good, consistent health plan. I try to do a couple of small things that have helped dramatically in the past few years. The first is planning my schedule so that I can eat at home more.

My family and I belong to several co-ops that provide organic meat, dairy, and vegetables. So eating at home usually means eating healthy—much healthier than grabbing a quick burger after that 6:00 meeting.

Second, we have to make time—I mean scheduling it as if it were a meeting—to exercise. I have the alarm set on my phone for every afternoon to tell me that I have a meeting, a meeting with the elliptical machine at the gym. Sometimes I hit ignore because I am in the sweet spot of mid-afternoon work, but more times than not I go to the meeting.

We have to discipline ourselves and schedule to make sure that these times are a priority. This is not so that we can be ready for the end of summer beach retreat, but so that when are old, graying, and have grandchildren our hearts will be vibrant and useful to play with those grandchildren. In a society in which 75 percent of its members are overweight and our number one cause of death is heart disease, it is also not a bad way to be counter-cultural in your student ministry.

5. Rehumanize Your Ministry

One of the most difficult things to do, especially in tough times, is to rehumanize our ministry. In a church culture that understands its success in terms of numbers, diversity of programs, and retention rate, it is easy to lose the fact that we are caring for individuals with unique lives, problems, loves, and passions. We often treat them and understand them like heads of cattle, constantly counting and recounting them and determining whether we have "fed" them the right food and the appropriate amount of growth is occurring. We have to remember, embrace, and celebrate that we are working with individuals with stories.

It is also so important and life-giving to place ourselves and understand what we do in the context of two thousand years of ministry and tradition. Sometimes we get bogged down in the trends and benchmarks of the past ten years—and, sometimes, the past ten months. We sometimes fool ourselves into believing that God is judging us on our annual growth percentages, diversity of programming, and weekly worship attendance. We are called into the business of loving people, making disciples, and witnessing to the life of Christ and the presence of God in and around us. You cannot chart that on a pie graph or detail that in an annual report.

How to Be Aware When You Are Unaware

Having people around you who are barometers of your well-being and priorities is very important. Sometimes, we work so diligently and are so focused on what we are trying to accomplish we forget to check the lights on the dashboard that alert us when our lives are lacking something important or are beginning to overheat. We all (A) need friends and loved ones who will love us enough to tell us when we seem to be pushing a little too hard, and (B) we must be willing to hear and accept their words when they are spoken. We cannot depend on always being self-aware enough to recognize this, which is why it is so important to have people surrounding us who can gift us with these warnings.

Vacation, Rest, and Play Are Appointments Too

There will be times in our ministries when we are just too busy. It just happens. It is good during these times to be faithful to the work we have committed to. We have to work diligently, we have to finish the job, but there also has to be a light at the end of the tunnel. Sometimes when we realize or someone points out to us that we are in a seasonal imbalance, we look ahead and cannot see the light of day. There has to be an end in sight in order to be able to work our way through our current imbalance. If, however, I could not see the break, I would be concerned and go through my calendar with a fine-toothed comb and eliminate some wonderful, but unnecessary, pieces of my work. Also, in the meantime, make sure to schedule your rest and play just like they were appointments with your senior minister. They are just as important. You do not have to tell others that you have your gym time or yoga scheduled, you just treat it like another meeting and allow other needs to fit into your schedule as available.

It is so important to remember that several seasons of imbalance equal an imbalanced life. Many of us, myself as well, have strung together 3–4 seasons of imbalance with a few weeks of respite in between each. We delude ourselves into believing that those are isolated times of imbalance. They are not. Balance should be the rule, not the exception. Most of us will get to a point when there is no lack of good and productive things that we are passionate about to involve ourselves in. The real measure of our life is not the number of good things we busy ourselves with, but more about the discernment we use when choosing the few that we will focus our lives around.

We Christians love our nine commandments. We love to quote them, put them on monuments, and even make old movies about them. Yes, we love the nine commandments... Yes, you heard me right, our *nine* commandments are really special to us. The reason I say "nine" is because we, especially those of us in student ministry, are notorious for almost always leaving one out. When Moses came down the mountain with the ten commandments, there was one that stood out as more counter-cultural and more peculiar than all the rest, and I would argue it still does today.

Walter Brueggemann in his book *Sabbath as Resistance* says that keeping Sabbath was so counter-cultural because it said to the world around it that these would be people who were not slaves to the gods of productivity and consumption. Even as we wear our crosses, sing our songs, and lead our student ministries, many of us (including myself, too often) find ourselves worshiping the god of production and not the peculiar God of Israel who tells us to slow down, rest, keep the Sabbath, and trust that everything else can wait.

Remember Your First Calling

At the end of it all, you cannot forget your first calling. Your calling to student ministry is not your first, and is not your most important. If you are parent or a spouse, that calling should always take priority over your calling as a minister. I have seen so many marriages break apart, children not know their parents, and ministers become completely isolated from their families because they place priority on their vocational calling above their calling to be spouses or parents. They cannot be your second priority. You must also remember that you are a child of God, and that is enough. So many of us feel the need to prove ourselves, to show ourselves worthy and be good enough. However, God has already taken care of that; there is no need for you to try to improve upon it.

Take care of yourself, your family, and your own spirituality, and goodness in ministry will surely follow.

No matter what you do in student ministry, do not forget that self-care is not a means to an end. Self-care is an end in and to itself.